A Mother's Nightmare

Also by Cathy Crimmins

Where Is the Mango Princess?

A Mother's Nightmare

A Heartrending Journey

into Near Fatal Childhood Illness

Cathy Crimmins

THOMAS DUNNE BOOKS
ST. MARTIN'S PRESS
NEW YORK

Author's Note: The names and identifying characteristics of some people have been changed.

THOMAS DUNNE BOOKS.
An imprint of St. Martin's Press.

www.thomasdunnebooks.com
www.stmartins.com

Library of Congress Cataloging-in-Publication Data

Crimmins, C. E.
A mother's nightmare : a heartrending journey into near fatal childhood illness / Cathy Crimmins. — 1st ed.
p. cm.
ISBN-13: 978-0-312-35781-8
ISBN-10: 0-312-35781-8
1. Crimmins, Kelly—Health. 2. Chronic active hepatitis—Patients—Pennsylvania—Biography. 3. Parents of chronically ill children. I. Title.
RC848.C4C75 2009
362.198'929780092—dc22
[B] 2009010674

First Edition: August 2009

10 9 8 7 6 5 4 3 2 1

For Kelly

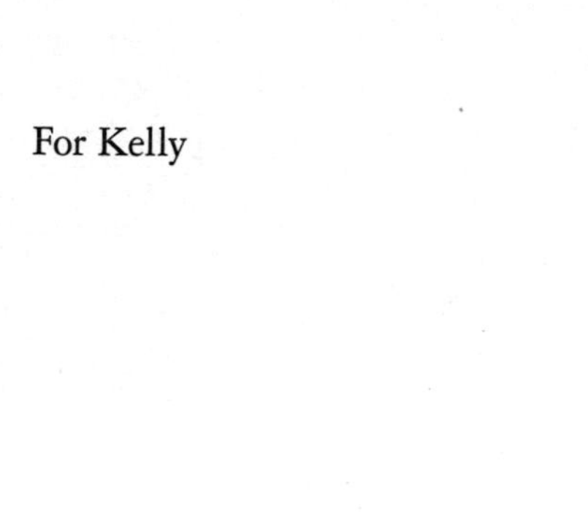

Contents

A Mother's Nightmare

Prologue

The Mother Speaks, or How I Became Sick Mommy

This has always been my big question: How does a woman describe her kid's grave illness without coming across as self-serving? How does the mother of a sick daughter ever come across well? It's a damned losing battle.

If she describes her struggle heroically, she seems boastful and disingenuous.

I hate that kind of mom. (Like, you're God's gift to the world just because your kid got sick!)

But, then again, if the mom is too human and lays out her frustrations and anger from the beginning, she becomes a shrew. (Of course this mother's kid got sick; she's full of rage! Look, she's pissed off at everyone! Maybe she even caused the illness!)

If the mom idealizes her daughter and is horrified by her illness simply because one should *always* be horrified by the suffering of the young and innocent, well—isn't that a bit Little Nell? A bit Dickensian? Because if the mom focuses on the physical side of her precious daughter's virginal strength, if she is constantly worried that her little, innocent girl has been invaded in her most private places, isn't that somewhat . . . *telling?* If the mom admits that she can't bear to think of her twelve-year-old with tubes sticking out her vagina, doesn't that say a little too much about the mom and her hang-ups? (And aren't vaginal tubes a bit too graphic for the reader?)

Face it: The whole presentation of the sick child situation is ripe with cultural stereotypes. "Don't be corny, Mom," Kelly always says. She's right. But how can you *not* be corny when the bad melodrama you awake to each day is like a *TV Guide* description of a Lifetime network movie?

> *Sick Mommy: Based on a True Story!* A mother and daughter endure endless hospitalizations only to discover the true meaning of life . . . (yeah, right).

> *Sick Mommy: Based on a True Story!* A mother fights for her daughter's rights in a brutal medical system, saving her from a rare and deadly liver disease . . .

> *Sick Mommy: Based on a True Story!* A mother kills herself because she realizes that her kid's disease has an 80 percent recurrence rate and she can't protect her from it, really, ever.

> *Sick Mommy: Based on a True Story!* A writer/mother never finishes writing the story of her daughter's liver disease, now in remission, because

she superstitiously believes that if she talks about it, it will happen again.

All of this stuff about having a sick kid is too horrible, and I can't win, really, in trying to tell this story. I know that. I know that however I present it, I'll look crazy. It seems so distant now, too, so distant that even I doubt that my child almost died.

But it's a fact.

Still, can I keep my credibility as a distraught parent while admitting that nowadays my eighteen-year-old kid has learned how to hate me with the verve and dedication she always lacked when she was so dependent in her illness? Now that she dislikes me so intensely, can I conjure up the emotional reality of fearing daily that she won't be around in a few months?

I can't, and yet I have to try. It's a natural compulsion, to fight off the bad stuff of the present by telling the crappy stories of the past. It's almost a relief now that my kid is a typical sullen teenager who despises me and sometimes even implies that I've made up this story of when she was a sick little kid and almost died.

People can tell you to get over your child's illness, to get on with your life, but you never do. Those who don't talk or write about it might seem as if they are over it, but, believe me, they're not. These people appear to me constantly, almost like the Ancient Mariners of children's deadly illness.

Take, for example, the guy who called me from the electric company.

One summer, six months after Kelly was diagnosed, we experienced a series of electrical disasters in the small backyard of our urban home. Actually, it was the culmination of many disasters. Our house, built in 1879, was part of one of the most ancient electrical grids in the city of Philadelphia. For three years in a row we'd been experiencing brownouts and blackouts during the deadliest hot days of summer. One time I dragged my husband, Alan, out to the street in his underwear after our VCR began flickering, only to find out that the electrical line feeding our house from the back alley had burst into flames, and all our neighbors were outside hoping we were still alive. Another time, after the electrical workmen had dug a hole to try to rewire something, the hole also burst into flames, looking a bit like an urban version of the burning bush in bad Moses movies.

So, this bad electrical karma had been flickering for a while when finally, the summer after Kelly was diagnosed with deadly liver disease, we had parts of a week with no power in our building at all, and indeed in the grid three blocks around it. Understandably, this became the buzz of the neighborhood, and down at the doggie park everyone was up in arms. Word was out that even PECO, the local electrical company, had realized how unfair our situation was and was willing to pay our expenses—the lost frozen and refrigerated food, and, when the heat became so unbearable, the cost of Kelly's and my spending the night at a Center City hotel.

"Make sure you go to a dog-friendly hotel so you can take Silver," Les at the dog park had said that afternoon, and I did, choosing the Loews Hotel down near Reading Terminal. It was swanky, and I worried that I'd never be reimbursed for it. But Kelly was very sick that summer—she'd been sent home from Girl Scouts sleepaway camp, and even with ice cubes and fans I couldn't get the house any cooler than ninety degrees. She was already feverish and suffering from kidney stone cramps, and I knew neither one of us would sleep much that night. The cats, with their mysterious ways, had exited the house through the upstairs hallway window and were probably languishing in some ivy bushes down along the lane. But Kelly, Silver, and I were suffering, so, at one in the morning, we filled the cat bowls with Meow Mix and set out to the hotel. I plunked down the requisite $125 and hoped for the best. At least the staff seemed to adore us in all our sweaty eminence, and Silver got great treatment, with a special package full of snacks and his very own Loews place mat and doggie bowl.

A few weeks later, long after our power was finally restored, I got a call from the electric company guy, a PECO negotiator. While it took me by surprise initially, I quickly tried to get hard-edged as he asked me how many refrigerated perishables I'd lost in the last blackout.

"Three hundred dollars' worth."

"Come on," he said. "You mean to tell me you were having that many electrical blackouts and you still kept that much stuff in your fridge?"

"Two hundred," I said.

"And it says here that you went to a hotel. How much did that cost you?"

"Over two hundred."

"I see."

"I had to go to a hotel, a good one. My daughter is seriously ill, with a rare liver ailment."

"Huh. Gee. Where is she a patient, at Children's?"

"Yes. CHOP. She has autoimmune hepatitis. AIH."

It was as if a switch had been turned on: My interrogator became my instant friend and ally.

"Children's was great to us. They really helped us with our son. Leukemia."

He went on to tell me that his son had been treated at a satellite of Children's in the Northeast. "His doctor is an amazing woman," he said. "I really love her."

"Oh," I said. "I'm so sorry you went through that. How is your son now?"

I didn't like the pause that came next.

"He didn't make it," the guy said, in a much smaller voice. "Not all of them do. Damn, though, she was a great doctor."

It didn't take much to make me cry in those days, and all of a sudden the tears were running down my face. The guy knew he'd stepped out of his professional bounds, and I felt awful for him on so many levels. Not only could he not believe he'd told me that his son was dead, but he probably couldn't believe that it had ever happened. When he left his cubicle at PECO to go home that evening, his little boy was not going to be greeting him in the driveway. Nor even his sullen teenaged son, the one who had recovered from leukemia and now didn't understand why his dad was so corny about it. In sharing his little boy's death with a stranger, had he cheapened it? Or had he told me something I needed to hear? Almost immediately, too, I took it as a sign—what if Kelly didn't recover, either? Was this strange guy on the other end of the line a messenger of some sorts? Was he preparing me for the worst outcome?

We relocated the conversational equilibrium in the only way we could, with him taking the lead. He turned hardball. If I thought I was going to scam him just because his kid had died of leukemia, then I was sadly mistaken.

"How much for the hotel again?" he asked.

"Two hundred," I lied.

"Listen, I can only give you two hundred for the whole thing."

"Okay," I said, relieved.

"I hope your daughter does okay," he said as he was hanging up. "Really, that doctor was swell."

When the tide was turning, and Kelly was beginning to despise me, only three years ago, she said that she had a title for my book, if I still wanted to write one. "Sick Mommy," she said. "Because my illness made you sick. Not me so much, but you. You were the sick one. My being sick made *you* crazy and sick."

She's right, of course, because kids should never get that sick. Such a cliché, but it's true. It's like that old bromide that the greatest tragedy of life is to have your child die before you. I think it's true, and it's why, if you ever face even the remotest possibility that your child will become sick and leave this earth before you do, you, too, will become a Sick Mommy.

1. The Mystery Illness

> The sick soon come to understand that they live in a different world from that of the well and that the two cannot communicate.
>
> *Jessamyn West*

What if I had known all along that it was going to happen? What if Kelly's disease hadn't come as a total surprise?

I ask myself this often, since, in retrospect, it makes sense that our only child developed an impossibly bizarre autoimmune disease.

Of course she did get terribly sick, and why not?

Bad things sometimes come in sequence, and our family had been suffering through a storm of bad things for some time. Based on the idea of bad things happening in numbers (threes?), I suppose I should have guessed that something was wrong with my daughter. At the time, all the signs were there that she was very ill, but I ignored them, maybe on the theory that lightning doesn't strike twice. I had my reasons to explain away anything bad—I had plenty of them, because denial had become my religion.

In the several years before Kelly became horribly sick, we had been anything but lucky. When Kelly was seven, her father, Alan, was struck in the head by a boat on a family vacation in Canada. The accident pretty much changed everything, plunging us into a nightmare world in which Alan became a child again. He had to learn all over again how to walk, talk, use the toilet. He returned to work as a lawyer in a bank but was fired after the first year because he never regained his physical or mental stamina. He was strange afterward, "like a new daddy, like he is wearing new skin," as then seven-year-old Kelly told me.

So, when Kelly got sick, we had been riding what experts call the roller coaster of traumatic brain injury for almost five years. Even though I'm sometimes forced to use the roller-coaster image myself when I talk to audiences about brain injury, I've come to resent it because the simile is too benevolent. I *like* roller coasters, damn it! Brain injury is *not* like a roller coaster, because most people have fun on a roller coaster, and no one has fun after brain injury. For the families of people with brain injuries, the experience is more like riding an elevator that is speeding up to the thirtieth floor and then suddenly stops and free-falls eight flights. It's not fun; it's terrifying. The floor is knocked out from under you, and you lose your wind. The families of brain injury survivors try very hard to regain some sort of normalcy, and there is a pattern we all follow as we try to pick up the pieces of our lives. Like so many brain injury survivors, our family felt blessed that Alan had triumphed physically over his accident, but then, when the initial terror and euphoria passed, we began to feel persecuted. The realization of how much we'd lost started to sink in. At around the time Kelly got sick, people at her school had started coming up to me and asking how I was able to cope with my new husband. It was beginning to sink in, even to the general public, that my cynical, edgy husband had become more like a sweet, slow-witted teenage son I had trouble managing.

People outside our family had no idea of our daily struggles, of how I'd have to defend our kid against Alan's outbursts and give my own husband "time-outs" in order to keep peace in the family. Our marriage was gone, and in its stead was an uneasy relationship I couldn't quite define. I was desperately lonely and out of control. An affair I thought could stay casual became my only ballast as I clung to whatever could get me through endless days and nights of terror. I was afraid of what had happened to Alan, too afraid to admit that most times I *hated* what had happened to him, to acknowledge that I was consumed with grief for the life we'd once had. Worse, I'd continued my writing career with a book about his brain injury and recovery, which cast me into a role I never wanted: the Brain Injury Martyr, the loving wife who is an inspiration to everyone around her. In truth I was full of rage and fatigue, adjusting to a husband who was like a sixteen-year-old boy. Most of all, I felt I was living a lie and that maybe I would be punished for it.

Was I punished for it? Is that why my daughter almost died—or would have if we hadn't caught her imploding liver in time?

No, that's too crazy to think, even for me. I sometimes practice magical thinking, but I draw the line at believing that I was a bad person who somehow *needed* a sick daughter to teach me something new about life. Yes, I was feeling damaged and vulnerable when Kelly's illness came along, but I was still remarkably surprised by what happened next. When she got sick, it felt as if she'd gone off and done it behind my back.

Moderately sick kids have always annoyed me, and unfortunately

I gave birth to a hypochondriac. When it came to sickness, Kelly was the girl who cried wolf again and again.

Before her major illness, Kelly never really got sick, but she was always pretending to be, magnifying minor colds into major incidents. In those days she was a real character, not above putting a thermometer next to a lightbulb or sticking her finger down her throat in an attempt to throw up before school. How could I have ever guessed that I, a mom who got pissed off even when Kelly got a case of the sniffles, would spend the next two years taking care of a kid who would almost die?

Nowadays I see what a stupid waste of energy it was on my part to resent Kelly's minor illnesses. She only wanted to exaggerate them so that she could spend time with me at home, but I never played the doting mom who enjoyed bringing her chicken noodle soup. Who were those chicken soup women, anyway? Didn't they have deadlines?

Luckily, Kelly was basically healthy before her autoimmune liver troubles began. She'd never had all those childhood ear infections or endless viruses that kept her friends under the weather. In her twelve years on earth, she had taken antibiotics only once, and her only serious illness had been a bout with giardia, a weird stomach parasite we'd all picked up by drinking "spring water" in the wilderness of Alberta, Canada, when she was two years old. Kelly was so healthy, in fact, that she never got sick enough to have to languish in bed all day. Even with a fever, she was a terror. Her energy level always remained high no matter what other symptoms she might be suffering. As soon as she could walk, her illnesses became mobile: Leave her alone in a room, and she would tear it apart. Vomiting took place on the run. I hated taking her to the pediatrician because of the endless waits in the examination rooms—they encourage you to get your kid naked and then leave you in a cold room with a naked toddler and no toys. It was all I could do to keep Kelly from destroying the medical equipment. The kid could be contained to bed only when I read to her or when I set up a portable TV to hypnotize her into a *Sesame Street* stupor. As a writer, I work at home, so having Kelly home sick from her preschool always meant a lost day.

Later, in the year that she was developing her liver disease, I was terrible about her requests to stay home.

"I feel tired, Mom," she'd whine.

"Of course you're tired—you never get enough sleep. Go to sleep early tonight, kiddo. If you think you're staying home because you don't go to bed early enough, you've got another thing coming."

"I have a stomachache," she'd say.

"Sure you do. It's from all the crap you ate last night. Get going, kid."

"I promise I won't bother you, Mom. Really. Please let me stay home."

"No way."

In the months before we found out that Kelly's liver was failing, she was getting skinnier by the week. (I just thought she was "thinning out," hitting adolescence with a vengeance.) And she was pale, but it was winter in Philadelphia, and everyone was pale.

So much for woman's intuition. I should have known! I should have known that my kid was on her way to dying. The evidence was mounting.

It only gets worse when I tell you about the Mystery Illness. How can I put the Mystery Illness out of my mind?

A year before Kelly's complaints of stomachaches and fatigue, we went to spend the millennium in Bangkok and Hong Kong, much to my mother's chagrin. Mom subscribed to all the dire predictions about Y2K: The world was going to end amid riots and war. At the very least, we were going to be without flashlights and bottled water over there in mysterious Asia while the world turned itself to a new century. She was furious with us; she didn't even call us before we left. In truth, the whole reason we were going on the trip was because most people my mother's age were terrified of Y2K. The trip was being sponsored by ABC Tours, which catered to an older crowd. In the weeks leading up to the flight, seeing that hardly anyone was signing up for it, the tour company had dropped the price each week by a few hundred dollars. By the time we signed up, it was as if they were paying *us* to usher in the year 2000 in Bangkok.

Our friends thought we were crazy. I remember one saying to me, "You're taking a ten-year-old and a brain-injured man to Asia?"

"Why not?" I said, trying not to notice that the idea was a bit crazy. "I'm gunning for a sequel."

This book is not a sequel, so let me just say this: The trip was one of the best things I've ever done. It was a magical family time. Kelly and Alan and I forgot all the crap we'd been going through as we ushered in the new millennium on the banks of the River Chao Phraya, gazing up at fireworks and feasting on sushi and pad Thai. Yes, Alan frequently got lost and bought hundreds of dollars' worth of very bad souvenirs, and Kelly was cranky in that way kids sometimes get overseas, but it was all worth it when we climbed on and around giant golden Buddhas and watched fishermen steadily working and monks bopping around us on motorbikes. It is a memory we'll have forever.

We might also have Kelly's shot liver as one of those memories, though, because three months after we returned and a year before she became desperately ill, she developed her short but troubling

Mystery Illness, the one that served as a prelude to her "real" liver disease.

I take back everything I ever said about how resilient Kelly was when sick. This thing knocked her on her ass to the point where she couldn't move for hours. Her fever was high and her bladder was seemingly so damaged that urine dribbled down her leg. She completely lost her appetite, and as a consequence, more than twenty pounds peeled off her frame within three weeks. Kelly had never been fat, but at that time she would never have been considered as having the ultimate preteen figure. One day, when her friend Jennifer came to visit, she complimented Kelly's new look.

"You are sooooo thin, Kelly," she said in her best Valley Girl tone. "Like, it's so cool."

"My mom always said I'd lose the weight without knowing it," Kelly said with more than a bit of pride in her voice.

Had I really said that to my daughter about her weight? I felt chastened. I was prescribing magical thinking for her figure concerns. Worse, I was endorsing the idea that losing weight when you became a teenager was a good thing. I made a mental note to say something about it, one that I threw into my brain's recycling bin almost immediately, because as Kelly's Mystery Illness lingered on, the weight loss became the least of my concerns.

For one thing, the poor kid seemed to have a very wicked bladder infection. I'd been prone to those as a teenager, too, and I felt awful for her. She had the usual high fevers and the chills and lethargy. But her fevers were not consistent: One hour she would be up over 101 and then a few hours later she would be in the low-to-normal range. At the time, we were seeing a general practitioner's group I hated—her dad had fallen in love with a particular GP right after his brain injury and had transferred all of us to his care. His practice was more like a public clinic than a private office, and what I particularly resented was that we often had to wait for hours to see a physician, and it was seldom the *same* physician. Alan saw it as a point of pride that we went to a clinic in West Philadelphia instead of to a "fancy" pediatrician in Center City Philadelphia—he even insinuated that I was a racist who didn't like waiting in an office full of black people.

I still believe that if we'd had a good pediatrician when this thing with Kelly started, we would have found some sane solutions much earlier on. It's another one of those things I beat myself up over. I often reflect on that time and wonder why I was so passive about our health care, and, besides laziness, I can say only that I often practiced passivity and opportunism when it came to child care. If I allowed Kelly to go to a doctor's office Alan loved, then he was more likely to take her there, and I could work longer hours. I'm nothing if not obsessive in my work, and I always hated all the routine child maintenance appointments—the school and camp examinations, the vaccinations, etc. Alan loved doing all that stuff, so I let him call the shots.

The first time Alan took Kelly to the doctor, they said she was suffering from a bad flu. The doctor on duty at the time wasn't concerned that she'd already been out of school for three days. These things take time, he said. I took her the second time and told the doctor about the fevers that came and went and her obvious signs of bladder infection.

The doctor, an attractive black woman with a nice bedside manner, suddenly turned to me and requested that I leave the room.

"Why?"

"I want to ask your daughter some things that she can answer on her own."

"I think I'll stay."

"I would prefer you didn't."

"I will stay."

The doctor was annoyed with me, and Kelly was getting fearful. The doctor moved toward the examination table and perched herself at the end.

"Now, Kelly, has anyone touched you who shouldn't touch you? Is there anyone in your house who hurts you?"

I felt my face get red. What the hell was this? My kid was eleven years old!

"No," said Kelly, looking at me quizzically.

"Kelly, have you had sexual intercourse with a boy?" said the doctor, gazing at her steadily.

"What?" Kelly looked even paler than she'd been. She looked over at me. I didn't know how I should arrange my face. I felt guilty when there wasn't any reason for me to feel guilty. I worried that the doctor would think I was sending signals to her, so I looked away. "I haven't even kissed a boy yet," Kelly blurted.

I giggled nervously, and the doctor smiled.

"Okay," she said. She sent Kelly out to a bathroom to get a "clean catch" urine sample and turned to me after the door had closed.

"You wouldn't believe how many kids we see who are sexually abused," she said, "and one of the signs is always the unexplainable bladder infection."

"Well, my daughter is not sexually abused, and she's not sexually active. It's horrible of you to suggest that she might be."

"It's standard practice," she said.

Kelly returned, got her clothes on, and we left for home, with me vowing never to see that particular doctor again. But how could I control it? I hated these big practices where you never made a personal connection with a caregiver. Worse, when I had told the doctor we'd been overseas in Asia, she didn't even note it down. Kelly's ailment had stretched on for days now, and I was beginning to worry that it was something more serious than a common virus or a simple bladder infection.

I don't know why they never cultured Kelly's urine. A week later I took her back to the office and got yet another doctor, who once again took a urine sample and said not to worry, that there was "something going around." By that time, Kelly had lost another ten pounds and was still spiking a 102 fever every other day. I complained to the male doctor that I'd been insulted by the previous doctor's questions about an eleven-year-old's sexual activity, and he also lectured me on the numbers of young girls who were abused. I wondered aloud if their methods really ever helped detect anything, and he just glared at me. Then we went home with a refill prescription for the sulfa antibiotic Kelly had been taking for almost ten days. When I called two days later to inquire about the results of the urine culture, I once again got the runaround. (Thinking about this infuriates me all over again, and I'm especially mad at myself: How could I have tolerated such a casual attitude toward my kid's test results? But life goes on—you know how it is. You make the phone calls, and you're upset, but then you have to let it go if you're going to get anything else done that day.)

About three days later, I'd had it with the Mystery Illness. Kelly, often too tired even to watch television, stayed in her room dozing on and off day and night. Her lethargy was what scared me most. She didn't even seem to have the energy to try to annoy me. It was a scary time, made more so because her dad couldn't understand my concern. He didn't see this illness as any different from the standard bad colds or viruses kids have throughout their childhood. Alan, especially after his brain injury, was a doting dad, and he rather seemed to enjoy Kelly being sick and dependent on us. While he wasn't with her all the time, he was in and out to his part-time jobs and enjoyed combing the city to buy her candy and stuffed animals to make her feel better.

The candy went uneaten, and it was getting harder to concentrate on my work. It was ironic—I finally had a sick kid who kept to herself and let me write, but my concentration was shot. "We took her to Thailand," I kept thinking, "and now she's dying of something mysterious." Alan and I had a friend, an artist, whose sister had volunteered in Thailand for the Peace Corps. After only a few months there she'd been sent back to the States to languish at a federal hospital for infectious diseases. She never regained her energy, our friend told us—the mysterious illness, never defined, changed her personality forever.

But our friend's sister had been out in the wildest areas of Thailand. By contrast, our trip to Thailand had been very "vanilla," I kept telling our friends. Mostly tours of temples in Bangkok, a trip on a luxury boat to some ruined Buddhist sites down the Chao Praya River, and one guided tour of a floating market.

"She's always putting her fingers in her mouth," my mom said one day while talking about Kelly on the phone to me. "You know she still sucks her thumb sometimes, even at eleven. God knows what got into her mouth." Memories of Kelly sitting low in the carved-out canoe boats at the floating market came to my mind—I saw her trailing her fingers in the water, and then eating the market's mangosteens.

I stopped telling my mom that Kelly was still sick. She was getting better, I told her—except that she wasn't. One afternoon I came down from my third-floor office to check on her. She was in bed, flat asleep on her back, a rare position for a girl who was usually casually tangled in the covers (we often called the sleeping Kelly "The Worm" because in the course of a night she could squirm around and steal a huge bed from any other sleeper). She looked corpselike, and when I touched her forehead, she was burning up. I freaked out and began tapping her.

"Get up. Get up! We're going to the hospital."

"Mommy? I'm tired. I have my pajamas on."

"That's okay. Stay in your pajamas. Wrap yourself in this blanket. Come on. I'm just going to put you into the car and we're going."

I'd been to the emergency room at Children's Hospital once before, when Kelly fractured her wrist at a soccer game, so I knew it was only ten minutes away. I couldn't get Alan—he was out wandering the city somewhere—but I knew it wouldn't be hard to get her there by myself. It was just a matter of finding our way from the parking garage to the emergency room.

Children's Hospital is filled with banners proclaiming that you're sitting in one of the top five children's hospitals in the country. I felt stupid as soon as we got there—was my kid really sick enough to justify an emergency visit? We had to park in the garage, which seemed a mile away, and I had to keep encouraging Kelly to move along in her pajamas and slippers.

The nurses didn't seem to think much of what was going on at the triage area, where they took Kelly's temperature and found it only slightly elevated. After charting her other symptoms, they sent us back to the waiting area's hard benches, where we cooled our heels for almost five hours before being called in. We'd arrived in the afternoon and now it was early evening. Alan had met us there and gone to fetch the junk food I would forever associate with Children's Hospital: McDonald's Happy Meals.

The waiting area for emergency at CHOP is in a huge atrium that was designed to be cheery but instead is very depressing: The high ceilings magnify every little sound, especially the pinging of the sadly abused interactive museum displays meant to delight the sick children waiting there. Every phone ring ricochets from the rafters, as do the computer printer sounds, the screams of unruly or vomiting children, and the annoying cash register sounds from the overpriced gift shop. And if the auditory delights don't get to you, there is the perpetual spectacle of very sick kids—hairless, emaciated, wrapped in bandages—being wheeled on gurneys from one procedure to the next, followed by anxious, hollow-eyed parents who haven't seen sunlight for weeks. That first day, waiting in that god-awful atrium, I thought of how lucky I was that Kelly wasn't an inpatient at the hospital. I had no idea that Alan and I would be following one of those gurneys only a year later, that the Mystery Illness would catch up to us eventually.

Eventually we were called in, and Alan and I recounted Kelly's medical history once again. I stressed to the interns our recent trip to Asia, and mentioned that she'd had the signs of a bladder infection but that our physicians had never gotten it together to culture her urine. The emergency team took a urine sample and then asked us to leave the room. Kelly was scared and said she didn't want me to go.

"We have to talk to this young lady *alone*," the attending female doctor said.

"Not this again," I said. "I assure you that my daughter is not sexually active."

"We'd like to ask her about that ourselves. It's hospital policy."

"She's eleven years old."

"Old enough."

I don't know what they would have done if I had truly refused to leave Kelly alone with them. I was tired and, after waiting five hours for anyone to pay attention to us, I certainly didn't want to wait another five to go through some procedural committee.

"Kelly, you'll be all right," I said, and left. I stood right outside and then made a point of coming back in after what seemed like a long five minutes.

"I told them again, Mom, that I haven't even kissed a boy," Kelly said. The doctor smiled but shook her head.

"Honey, you're getting older. We just have to ask these things." She began pushing on Kelly's abdomen. "When did you last go to the bathroom?"

"You mean poop?"

"Yes. Kelly, when did you last have a bowel movement?"

"I can't remember," said my kid, suddenly embarrassed.

"She hasn't been eating much of anything," I said.

"Well, Kelly, you've got a lot of hard poop in there. That might be why your stomach hurts."

They sent Kelly for an ultrasound, which did show accumulated fecal matter in her colon. "High level of constipation," said the doctor. Kelly's eyes watered as the technician pressed the Doppler wand, hard, on her lower abdomen.

But then a curious thing happened: Kelly's blood tests came back and her liver numbers were way off. Her AST number—for aspartate aminotransferase, a chemical the liver uses to make glycogen—was over five hundred (the regular reading is supposed to be under fifty). CHOP was concerned enough to send around a liver specialist, who said it was highly unusual for a child to show such high liver numbers.

"Are you sure they're not *my* liver numbers?" I said, attempting a stupid joke.

It could be the fever, said the hepatologist—a high fever can sometimes make liver numbers go screwy—or it could be hepatitis A or B. He was the only doctor who seemed at all interested that we'd recently been to Asia. "But the window of time for contagious hepatitis is well past; you would have seen it before this four-month period," he said. Still, he ordered tests, and I was advised to tell Kelly's baby-sitter that she might have been exposed to some sort of mystery hepatitis.

We went home with a notepad full of instructions for giving our child over-the-counter laxatives and stool softeners. It had been more than nine hours, and all we'd found out was that our kid was constipated. It all felt silly.

Even though the CHOP liver doctor advised our following up the next day to see if Kelly's liver numbers had gone down, when I told our pediatric practice this, they said it really wasn't necessary, that there was nothing to worry about—it was definitely the fever that was elevating the liver numbers. They believed this even more after all Kelly's tests for contagious hepatitis came back negative.

I took comfort in what the liver doctor, the most communicative one of the CHOP team, had said to me: "I'm sure Kelly didn't pick up anything in Thailand or China. Remember, we have hepatitis breakouts here, too—there was that recent one in Michigan, for example, with the contaminated strawberries."

So I wasn't a bad mom, after all.

In the days that followed it was as if taking her to the hospital turned out to be the magic cure—her fatigue lessened, her fever let up, and she returned to school skinny enough to wear the shorter "tummy tops" she'd been eyeing ever since she'd started edging toward adolescence.

Of course, now I know that the Mystery Illness was just a dress rehearsal for the Big One. It had all the elements—surprise, frustration, hopelessness—that Kelly's later real illness would come to embody, and yet it seemed like a problem that had gone away. We had almost another year before Kelly got so sick that she almost died, and I can't help but feel that if I had been worth my salt as a mother, I wouldn't have been so complacent. I might have pressed my questions about why her liver was going kablooey. I might have wondered more ardently why a healthy, active kid had suddenly become lethargic and anorexic. At the very least, I would have insisted on the pediatrician taking urine cultures. But life is busy, and I had dozens of deadlines, and Alan and I were beginning to struggle toward a marital separation, so I had plenty of other things to occupy my mind. Right before the Mystery Illness, Kelly had gotten her first period, so I was even able to chalk up the incident to the onset of puberty. The loss of appetite, the fatigue, and even the weight loss all added up to one amazing and rather vicious lurch toward womanhood.

Recently, Kelly and I were sitting around talking to our new neighbors in Los Angeles about the subject of this book, and she remembered the Mystery Illness as just vanishing, too. But what I didn't know, until my sixteen-year-old daughter told me in front of our neighbors, was that the second phase of her illness started soon afterward.

"But right after that," she said, "I started peeing funny, and that's one thing I never told my mom about. I don't know why, but maybe I was embarrassed, or maybe I just thought it was normal. It wasn't like I had blood in my urine back then, it was more like, well, dark beer. The pee that came out of me was always really dark. Now, when I look back at it, I can't believe I didn't tell my mom, but I guess I thought I was grown up and wanted to be private, or that I thought it would go away."

Oh, how I wish it had gone away!

2. The Diagnosis

What a difference a day makes,
Twenty-four little hours . . .

song by María Méndez Grever and Stanley Adams

I used to love the song with that title—my friend Tom gave me Dinah Washington's recording of it, and for a few months, in my thirties, I saw it as my constantly optimistic anthem.

It's true that no matter how much we see life as a huge block of time that sprawls before and after on an unrelenting continuum, there are moments, and hours, and days, that change everything for either the better or the worse. I had a hard time absorbing this when it came to Kelly's illness. The only model I had for it was Alan's accident, and an accident is something that happens *immediately*. First your husband is fine, and then only minutes later he is in a coma because a boat hit him on the head. No doubt about it, there is a cause and a consequence; it's hard to take, but easy to understand.

Yet with Kelly's illness, time acted almost the same way, even though it's taken me more than five years to admit it. One day my kid was healthy, and the next she was a hospital patient. And the hours it took to get from one condition to the next had that same eerie quality as the time around an accident—it seemed abrupt and gradual all at once.

I look back at the week before Kelly's diagnosis and wonder how I lived through it—which is stupid, because I didn't know my child was about to be diagnosed with a deadly disease, so of course I had no trouble living through the time right before it. In fact, it was a pretty good time.

We were in the midst of a fairly mild Philadelphia winter, and on Kelly's twelfth birthday, February 5, 2001, she opted to have a small party for her adult friends. (I guess that Kelly is a fairly typical only child, in that she's thought she was thirty years old since she was three.) We ordered her favorite takeout food, Vietnamese, and a nice ice-cream cake.

There were the usual suspects: six grown-ups who had been close to Kelly from birth, single people without children who love to spoil our kid rotten. It was a tumultuous time in our lives—Alan had moved out of the house a few months before. But of course he was there for her birthday party—our split has always been amicable—and we had fun singing and eating. I think all of us wanted to be reassured that we were still a family, no matter what crap had come down on us in the months before then.

Kelly's illness hit me hard, but I always wonder if I would have been better able to deal with it if I hadn't spent the last five years dealing with Alan's accident. After getting over the scariness of the coma, we'd had to deal as a family with his personality changes and mood swings. And I'd had to cope with our horrible insurance policy, which featured the deadly "gatekeeper" system, which had required me to fight at every step of the way to get him the rehabilitation services he needed. By the time Kelly got sick, I was burned out. I'd completed enough pages of insurance forms to have written a Tolstoy novel. Plus there was the strain of constantly trying to explain to friends and neighbors that while Alan looked the same, he'd had severe frontal lobe damage that had altered his personality for life. As recoveries go, Alan's recovery from brain injury was amazing.

He was a brilliant man—we'd met as graduate students of an arcane subject (medievalism), and after the educational job market had bottomed out in the early eighties, he'd gone to law school. We led an almost enchanted life for quite a while—lots of friends, many parties, and many shared interests that gave us joy. We attended the Philadelphia Orchestra and had subscriptions to many local theater groups. Whenever we could, even after Kelly's birth, we would sneak away for a weekend to gorge ourselves on Broadway shows. I think some people hated us, and I don't blame them, now that my life has shrunk down considerably—those heady years in our thirties now seem like a Paradise Lost. With an only child, we were much more able to keep our lifestyle fairly similar after Kelly's arrival—she went to her first musical when she was three, and began going to dramas in New York when she was seven. I used to joke that we'd had a child to make sure we had a constant movie and theater companion. We were lucky in those days, and everything seemed to go our way, until that fateful vacation when Alan got hit on the head by the speedboat. Since his accident and Kelly's illness, I've learned that we should all celebrate the nice surprises in life, since you never know when a really bad one might be lurking around the corner.

I had been in love with Alan since 1977, and I remained in mourning for his old self for years (to be honest, I am still in mourning for the old Al, whose personality was reconstituted when that boat hit his head in 1996). When Kelly got sick, I experienced a whole new surprising wave of mourning, because I knew that Alan, who now had the judgment skills of a sixteen-year-old, would never be able to help me manage our daughter's illness. I felt unbelievably lonely, and too helpless to offer much comfort to my child. The timing was terrible: Alan and I had been separated only three months when Kelly's AIH was diagnosed. Could I put my child through even more stress?

That day, at Kelly's twelfth birthday party, my mother pulled me aside. "What's wrong with Kelly?" she said. "She looks really pale, washed-out."

I assured her that Kelly was just turning into a teenager. The fact that she'd lost over twenty-five pounds a year ago and kept it off didn't concern me; she was losing her baby fat. She was indeed on the threshold of womanhood, and would excitedly talk to me in bed late at night, before she fell asleep, "Mom, you said it, and it's come true—I just lost the weight, automatically. Just like you said." Kelly had never been heavy, but she'd never been skinny, either. Now she had attained that Kate Moss look, and she wasn't starving herself. Every shopping expedition was a joy, as she discovered teen clothes that fit and looked "awesome."

One thing did concern me: She had started menstruating, and then she stopped. At the time of her twelfth birthday, it had been over a year since she'd had her period. I asked other mothers about this, and then a few doctors during checkups. A disrupted menstrual cycle is very common in young girls, I was told by both doctors and moms.

How could I not have known that Kelly was so sick?

Because we'd already had the Mystery Illness, and I guess I was desperate to think that nothing else would happen.

Yet there were a lot of signs that her health was in jeopardy. For starters, my mother was right: Kelly was preternaturally pale. I'm a light albino-type person, but Kelly had always been able to tan; we used to joke that she got Alan's Eastern European swarthiness, not my pale Irish genes. I have baby pictures that show her ruddy complexion. She'd also developed an odd case of acne, small pimples over her cheeks. I later found out that this type of tiny, masklike acne indicates liver disease. At the time I thought she was just getting adolescent pimples. And she often complained of constant itchiness, another symptom. Who knew? I thought she just had a case of dry winter skin. The symptoms kept piling up. For about three months before she was diagnosed, she often was tired and had stomachaches. But her total energy never flagged, as it had during the Mystery Illness the year before, so I never let her use her symptoms as an excuse to stay home from school. I'm ashamed now of the times I yelled at her, "Get out of bed! You're not sick! You're going to school!"

But she *was* sick.

The week after her birthday, still not knowing, I flew to Cleveland to give a speech about brain injury at the children's facility of the famous Cleveland Clinic, a rehab place where they treat many pediatric brain injuries. Everyone was delightful. I often give lectures, and sometimes they're just routine. But at special places, such as the

Cleveland Clinic, people go out of their way to welcome you. The clinic staff had arranged for me to stay in an elegant bed-and-breakfast across from the Case Western business school campus, where a new Frank Gehry building was going up. (He's the architect who designed the Disney Concert Hall in Los Angeles and the now-famous Guggenheim Bilbao.) Lots of wavy stainless steel. That morning in Cleveland, I was excited to watch a Gehry construction in process.

And it just got better as the day went on. At the dinner before my speech, the catering staff had created a banquet with dishes made of mangos. (The title of my book, *Where Is the Mango Princess?,* was something Alan had said when he came out of his coma.) So we ate mango and avocado appetizer, mango chicken, mango cake. The speech was well received, and I met some wonderful people who'd raised money for the rehabilitation center, many of whom had children with brain injuries.

I flew back to Philadelphia on Valentine's Day feeling great about my presentation. My boyfriend met me at the airport with roses. Eleven roses, as Kelly later remarked, after counting them in the vase on the dining room table.

"There probably were a dozen there before." Kelly said, deadpan. "He gave one of them to his other girlfriend." She hated my boyfriend, and I didn't blame her. She didn't understand all the stresses my marriage had been through after the accident, and my boyfriend had no idea how to woo an eleven-year-old. It was a disaster in the making. He was the kind of man who needed copious amounts of attention, and eventually, months later, when I had to decide between this man and Kelly, I chose Kelly.

Kelly could always crack me up. She did wicked impressions of my boyfriend. I knew I should have reprimanded her, and sometimes

I did, but most times I couldn't resist laughing. She is a natural parodist, always inventing names and shorthand descriptions. The comedy writer in me has always marveled at her gift for mimicry. She called my boyfriend "Sock Man," saying that he looked like a sock puppet.

But that's the thing about Kelly: People would always say things such as "She's a pip" or "She's a soul who's gone around a few times." As soon as she got sick, I worried about that all the time. Was her soul going to turn around fast this time? Were we going to lose her?

Sometimes I get really superstitious and think I curse myself. On the plane back from Cleveland, I'd had one predominant thought: As awful as Alan's accident had been, and as difficult as our family's struggle with his brain injury had been, I couldn't imagine having a sick kid. A sick husband is one thing, but a child who became ill when she had her whole life ahead of her? It made me shudder to think about it. The people I'd met at the Cleveland Clinic seemed so courageous, managing their children's illnesses, and I wondered if I could ever face such a challenge.

The very next day, when Kelly came home from school, she told me the news that would once again turn our lives upside down.

"Mommy, I've been peeing blood."

She said this as if she were asking me to fill out a permission form for a class trip.

"Peeing blood? There's blood in your urine?"

She nodded.

"How long?" I said.

"For a while now."

"Weeks?"

"A couple of months."

Wow. This was a big surprise, and not only because there was blood in her urine. I was surprised at how old she was now, and how I no longer saw her urine every day. She peed, she flushed. She was becoming autonomous in the way that all moms crave and fear at the same time. I felt guilty and far away from my own child. If she had been a toddler, or even in kindergarten, I would have known the intimate secrets of her body. I might have spotted her illness earlier.

The rest of that afternoon was a blur of anxiety. Kelly didn't seem too concerned about the blood, but she must have been worried on some level, because she had finally told me about it. She said she was sure it wasn't her period. No, the blood was coming from another place, she said, and it wasn't staining her underpants. She went to the bathroom again, and I asked her not to flush the toilet.

I gasped when I saw its contents. Her urine was bright red. I guess I had expected it to be copper-colored, but no, this crimson mess made it look as if a fork were stabbing her bladder.

We had dinner. Alan was over that night, too, to eat with us, as he did at least three times a week. At one point I took him aside to say that something was wrong, but he was very tired and I wasn't sure I was getting through to him. His brain injury made it difficult for him to focus on what I was saying.

I waited until he had gone home and Kelly had escaped to do her homework, then I climbed up to my office on the third floor and began to freak out. I called my boyfriend, who was a medical researcher. He knew a lot of doctors in town.

"Can you get me a sample?" he said.

"I think so."

Isn't it weird how people like to do melodramatic things when a crisis occurs? I still wonder why I didn't just drive Kelly to the emergency room at Children's Hospital that night. Why did I choose to go this labyrinthine route, of giving my boyfriend a cup of my kid's brilliant red urine in the early evening, on the streets of Philadelphia?

His plan was to get the urine to a friend who had once been a department head at a hospital. He had a lab in his basement and could tell us instantly if there was something serious going on. Two major egos were involved. First, there was my boyfriend, one of the most astute medical researchers. He desperately wanted to prove himself. He wanted to be involved, even if Kelly hated him. He believed he could cut red tape for me, and get her diagnosed immediately. That was a relief. And then there was the doctor—I'll call him Dr. Arrowsmith. This medical researcher missed having a practice. He missed the excitement of diagnosis. He missed it enough to jump at the chance to look at my daughter's urine later in the evening in his basement.

The whole operation seemed like a drug deal, or a spy mission. First, I managed to persuade Kelly to pee in a cup, saying we would take the sample to the doctor the next day. Then I stood near the back alley of our house in the crowded central part of the city, waiting with a Tupperware container of my kid's bloody pee. It was warm for a February evening, and my faithful terrier, who barely ever left my ankle, was standing with me. As luck would have it, the neighborhood psycho lady whose dog liked to attack other dogs passed by and, in the words of a sitcom synopsis, "mayhem ensued."

Her dog lunged and barked at mine, my dog snarled back, and then the psycho lady (who had never said a word to me the whole time), began kicking my dog and screaming. I retreated into the lane behind my house, with a panting dog and a urine sample that hadn't spilled, thanks to the wonders of the Tupperware seal. I'd wanted to yell at the lady: "Hey, my kid is really sick! She might have cancer or something! Can't you spare me the doggy drama for one night?" But she said nothing, and neither did I.

The beginning of Kelly's diagnosis was a tragicomedy, very undignified. There was no kindly family doctor such as the ones you see in the better movies about medicine. Maybe that's why I was panicky—way too panicky to wait to see such a doctor, or even to want to get Kelly to an emergency room. I wanted Dr. Arrowsmith to take over.

My boyfriend took the sample and fled to the suburbs, to Dr. Arrowsmith's basement laboratory. A few hours later, he called my boyfriend with bad news. Then I talked to Dr. Arrowsmith himself, who explained it: The blood in Kelly's urine had "castings" in it. That meant that it was coming from Kelly's kidneys, and not from a more superficial bladder infection. Dr. Arrowsmith called a friend, a kidney specialist (nephrologist) and the head of his department at the hospital, and got us an appointment for first thing the next morning.

Dr. Arrowsmith, who had three daughters of his own, was supportive. "Don't worry," he said right before hanging up. "Your daughter is going to be okay." I knew he was just saying it, though.

I spent the night tossing and turning, thinking about all the terrible consequences of kidney disease. Were my kid's organs failing? I imagined her on dialysis, with her growth stunted. And as the night drew on and my insomnia sharpened, I imagined her dead.

I wish I could remember what I told Kelly when I woke her up extra early the next morning to tell her she wasn't going to school that day. I know I didn't tell her I'd given her bloody urine sample to the Boyfriend, because she would have freaked out. Instead, as quickly and vaguely as I could, I said that we were going to take some of her urine to the doctor's, that I'd gotten a special appointment.

Kelly was tired and hazy, so it was easy to dupe her. She never even asked where her original sample was. She seemed to realize that whatever was happening, it was serious, because I was the one taking her to the hospital, not her dad.

We were lucky to have these flamboyant medical characters as part of our family drama. Most people must wait hours, days, weeks, even months to find out what is wrong with their child. And if I hadn't known already that we were privileged, I certainly realized it the next day, when we were ushered through a crowded waiting room at the Children Hospital's kidney clinic and into Dr. Jones's office. I could barely look into the eyes of the anxious parents who watched us walk by and enter the inner sanctum.

Dr. Jones made some funny comments about the secret derring-do that had led us to his office. He was a nice, gentlemanly guy in his sixties with a charming accent. I was impressed that he succeeded in making small talk with Kelly, who at this point was startled by how quickly she had become a "sick girl." The doctor wasn't sure that castings were present in Kelly's urine samples, but he said that there was definitely something wrong. He sent us for an abdominal ultrasound to see if Kelly's kidneys were in working order, and ordered more blood tests. Kelly also provided him with another urine sample, since, the doctor said, winking, "the last sample was not exactly produced or stored under sterile conditions."

It was the ultrasound technician who first hinted that something was seriously wrong.

"There's her spleen," she said, running the gloppy Doppler wand over Kelly's stomach. "It's much too big. I've never seen this in a kid."

The kidney doctor confirmed the technician's comments: "Kelly's spleen is greatly enlarged—three times its normal size," he said. Her blood test also looked bad. Once again, as with the Mystery Illness of the year before, her liver function numbers were high. But this time they were off the charts. An average liver function number is, say, thirty, and Kelly's measured in the thousands. Oddly enough, her kidneys looked normal on the ultrasound, the nephrologist said.

"What does an enlarged spleen mean?" I asked.

"It could mean any number of things," the doctor said quietly. At the time, I didn't get how scary his subdued demeanor was. "Her bile ducts might be blocked in some way, or there might be some liver involvement. I've found an excellent diagnostician, a young doctor who works a lot with unusual liver conditions. I want you to go right over to her office. I'm giving you this file, and this letter. Don't let anyone turn you away. You're to see her immediately."

Immediately is bad in a hospital, especially in a large urban hospital.

And now we had to go *immediately* to the gastroenterology

department, the department covering digestive and liver ailments. When all this began, I could barely pronounce the word. By the time we were a year into our medical adventure, *gastroenterology* tripped off my tongue.

Clutching all our documents and the enormous folder with the ultrasound films, I guided Kelly through the hospital maze to the department where they focused on the liver. We went up one floor, down one floor, and through a glass bridge of the type that almost all hospitals have. The walk felt like forever. With each step, I wasn't feeling the floor. My kid was sick. What the hell did she have? I looked over at her and wanted to carry her, but she had been too big for that for at least six years. I considered getting a wheelchair, since all of a sudden she seemed very fragile.

Amazingly, our on-the-brink-of-death letter from the kidney doctor got us in to see the liver doctor, or gastroenterologist, immediately. Dr. Palmer was a stern-looking woman in her late thirties with her long hair pulled back in a bun. I didn't start out hating her right away—but it came naturally after a few months. She was the one to break the really bad news to us.

"We're not totally sure," she said, "but it looks as if your daughter has one of two liver diseases. It could be Wilson's disease, or another rare illness, autoimmune hepatitis. Wilson's is easier to cure. Autoimmune hepatitis is a rather rare condition in which the body attacks the liver. We can't be sure until we do a liver biopsy. But all the symptoms indicate AIH."

The liver is more vulnerable than we think, and many diseases or conditions can destroy it quite quickly. But not all of them are created equal. Some liver conditions are deadlier than others. I knew a little about Wilson's, a weird disease that comes about when the body can't process copper. With a Wilson's patient, you see a brown glow in the eyes. The excess copper in the blood mounts up in the body and eventually lands in the liver, causing damage. Wilson's is just odd, yet understandable, enough to have become a recent favorite on medical TV shows. I've noticed it cropping up on *ER*, *House*, and even one of the *CSI* programs. A simple blood test for copper levels is all it takes to diagnose Wilson's, but obviously the kidney doctor hadn't done more than basic liver function tests. Now this young gastroenterologist would test further to discover the secrets of Kelly's dying liver.

With all the horrid possibilities for Kelly's condition, Wilson's would have been a blessing. How odd, I thought, to find myself wishing that my child had a hereditary inability to digest copper. But I knew that in the spectrum of possible liver diseases, Wilson's was a walk in the park.

The other and more likely disease, autoimmune hepatitis (AIH), was much, much scarier, yet this was the diagnosis Dr. Palmer was leaning toward. That first day in the gastroenterologist's office, I learned that the word *hepatitis* merely meant inflammation of the liver. Hepatitis A, B, and C are all contagious, but AIH is not—it is the result of the body turning on itself. To put it simply, the blood cells go wild and try to destroy the liver. In the 1970s, autoimmune hepatitis was called "lupus of the liver," and by the 1990s, two types had been identified. We would be lucky if Kelly had Type 1; the second type was much more difficult to treat.

By the time we were finished talking to Dr. Palmer, it was about eleven A.M. She convinced us that the best thing to do was an emergency admission, right then and there. The next day, Kelly could have all the tests she needed, including more imaging and a liver biopsy.

Wow, were we naive. Sure, I knew that getting treated in an

emergency room took hours, but I thought that an emergency admission recommended by a doctor would be much simpler and faster. It seems silly now, because we lived only ten minutes from the hospital and could have gone home to fetch anything we needed, but I was in a panic. I never thought about anything else but getting Kelly's sick tushie into a bed as soon as possible. I somehow thought that if she never left the hospital, she wouldn't be in danger of dying. It was the first onset of my many magical-thinking episodes.

The admission to the gastroenterology floor took almost six hours. First, while Kelly sat on a narrow bed in the emergency area, I filled out forms that already seemed too familiar after only half a day of dealing with the hospital. Why do hospitals take your history every time you check in? I told every emergency doctor about the Mystery Illness the year before, but no one seemed to care. I told every doctor that we'd been to Thailand right before the Mystery Illness. No one made note of it. Or at least none of those comments ever seemed to make it into Kelly's charts. *Mother is too imaginative*, I later imagined them writing. Of course, that exact phrase never appeared, either.

It was dark by the time they got Kelly into a room. She was exhausted and hungry, and the early hospital dinners had already been delivered and cleared. My mother had arrived shortly before, rushing down from her house outside the city, about an hour away. She encouraged me to go home for a little while, so I did, planning to grab some sweatpants, snacks, and a quilt for Kelly's bed. Grandma had come armed with snacks and small talk, so Kelly didn't protest too much when I took off for home.

Going home without Kelly seemed strange, and when I saw our

little dog inside the front door, I felt guilty that I had no tenderness for him. I shoved his food into a dish and some things into bags and rushed right out again. I couldn't stop to walk a dog while my child was languishing in a hospital bed, waiting to have her liver punctured. I had to get back as soon as possible, and even though it felt like an eternity, I was away from Kelly for only forty minutes. I stopped by our corner store to pick up some prepared food for her and my mother. Again, this seemed like a familiar, mundane task, but I could barely keep from crying while doing it. I wanted to tell all the people at the store that Kelly was very sick, in the hospital. But I said nothing.

Kelly was uncomfortable and cranky when I returned, and Alan was there looking confused and upset. The whole day had been a bizarre, almost exciting adventure, but now Kelly was realizing that she would actually have to stay in the hospital. Every symptom of liver failure she'd heard about from the doctors seemed to be plaguing her now. She was itchy, and her stomach hurt. She was finally beginning to understand that she would have an operation in the morning. Because she was a big twelve-year-old, they couldn't find her a hospital gown that fit; she had to wear nurse's scrubs. At least the quilt and blanket I'd brought helped. In fact, if I could give one piece of advice to the parents of a sick child in the hospital, it would be this: Bring familiar-looking bedding. The child will be comforted, and the nurses will be so shocked to see something interesting looking, they'll comment on it frequently. Our thirty-five-dollar discount store quilt got as many compliments as a handmade heirloom would have.

All around us on the gastroenterology floor, babies were crying. It seemed strange that patients were grouped by disease rather than age. The infants with faulty digestive systems and livers were screaming throughout the wing, and the older kids had to try not to listen.

When I went out to the ice machine that first night, I passed a room where a frail one-year-old was having blood taken. I looked in, feeling like one of those people who stop to watch car wrecks. The screaming baby's parents were holding her down by her little stick arms while the nurse wielded the needle. What a terrible thing, I thought, to watch someone hurt your infant, and to feel complicit in the act. At least Kelly understood that she was sick. I could talk to her about it.

The little girl in the bed next to Kelly was very ill. Her parents were going through a worse nightmare than ours. Their son and daughter had suddenly fallen ill at the same time and had to be rushed by ambulance to the hospital. For the boy, who was ten and was on another floor in the intensive care unit, hooked up to all sorts of machines, it was touch-and-go. The girl, Kelly's roommate, was eight. Her liver was in failure, too, but not to the extent of her brother's. The parents took turns with the kids, switching places to make sure that someone was always with each child.

The Father, a heavy-set, balding man, was hysterical that first night, yelling at any nurse or doctor he could find. I didn't blame him. "What the hell are all these tests about," he said, "if we still don't know what is wrong with my kids?"

The hospital attendants responded patiently to his bellowing: Tests take time; we are trying to make your children comfortable, etc.

I wanted to bellow along with him. How the hell had this happened? Why was my once-healthy child a basket case? How had our whole family entered hell overnight?

I call this man the Father, but I suppose it's only natural, since everyone at Children's Hospital started calling me the Mother.

"And what does the Mother think?" almost every doctor would ask when he or she came around to examine Kelly. "Is this the Mother?" "Has the Mother given us a history?"

And in the hospital charts, you are just "Mother," as in, *Mother seems overly concerned,* or, worse, *Mother is uncooperative.* I don't think there are as many entries for "Father."

After I gave birth, I hated losing my first name. I was no longer Cathy. To everyone in the neighborhood and at Kelly's preschool I became "Kelly's mother." One gives in rather early on this topic—I soon found myself calling other parents to arrange toddler playdates and identifying myself as "Kelly's mom." But it never felt right.

The hospital identification process was worse, though. You lose the child's given name, too. They can't even keep track of that.

When Kelly was admitted to Children's Hospital that day, the security desk issued me a plastic identity bracelet, and later the guards at the desk gave one to Alan, too. The Mother and the Father bracelets. I figured out a way to slip mine off, because it irritated my wrist to the point of a rash. The rash was definitely psychosomatic. If I had been wearing such an ID bracelet to gain entrance to the buffet at a Caribbean resort, I'm sure my skin wouldn't have reacted that way.

You had to flash the bracelet to the security guards, identifying yourself as someone who had A Very Ill Child, and then they'd let you pass through the barrier. It was a perverse version of getting into an exclusive club, only this one offered nothing but sorrow and pain.

As Kelly's nurse showed me the pullout cot where I would sleep that first night, I was in shock. I'd already called many of our friends, talked to my mom and Alan, and answered scores of questions about Kelly's condition from technicians, nurses, and physicians—but nothing was sinking in except the feeling of dread that something had gone terribly wrong.

One day your child is fine, and the next day she's not. It's very hard to absorb. You find out that her spleen is enlarged to three times its normal size. That she has the cirrhotic liver of a hardened alcoholic. That she most likely is in stage four of liver failure (with five being the end). That she might have a disease so rare you've never heard of it. It's an autoimmune disease, which means that her body is destroying itself. (What a potent metaphor. Why would her preadolescent body want to die?) All the nurses and attending doctors ask if there is autoimmune disease in your family. There is not, but the blame still feels like yours. And when you wake up the next day, the news is still there.

Two doctors and four nurses at CHOP have already asked if Kelly was a premature baby. No. Was she underweight at birth? No. Damn, she was big. Eight pounds, nine ounces. The night Kelly was born, I watched Cary Grant movies. I hung out in a Jacuzzi, laboring without drugs at a hippie birth center. I was so smug then. Our daughter was born perfect.

But in the end it didn't matter what I said to any of the hospital inquisitors. It was twelve years later, and Kelly was no longer a robust baby. She was not healthy. It didn't mean anything that she'd taken antibiotics only once in her first decade of life. It didn't matter that she was a star athlete in the fifth grade. She was sick now. And now the people around you at the hospital are the ones who seem smug. They know the truth: Your child can't be the healthy baby/child you're pretending she is. She is very ill. How could she ever have been healthy? How could you, the Mother, not notice what has become of her?

Kelly's nurse on the gastroenterology floor was young and nice, and that first night she went out of her way to flatter Kelly and try to bond with her. She even admitted that she hadn't been on the job long. After she told me about the library of videotapes in the special family center where I could go take a shower, she pulled out yet another lifestyle questionnaire. I couldn't believe I had to answer more questions; the admission process had taken nine hours from start to finish and it was already after nine P.M.

The nurse filled in the questionnaire for me, as if I couldn't possibly have completed it myself. There were dozens of weirdly worded, insulting questions, such as, "Is your child subject to domestic abuse in your household?"

At one point, the nurse smiled sweetly and read this question: "How long have you known about your daughter's *terminal* illness? Have you talked to her about it?" And she says this in front of Kelly.

Terminal. There is a vast silence after she says it.

"Terminal?" I squeaked. "Have you been told something I don't know?"

The nurse looked down at the form on her lap. "Oh geez, did I say *terminal*?" Her voice sounded upset. "What she has is probably *chronic* liver disease. Oh, like, I am so sorry. I meant *chronic*. Really. I misread it."

We continued filling out the form. But the word *terminal* had been thrown out there, like the first pitch of a softball game. I almost felt thankful for the nurse's mistake because she had inadvertently voiced my worse fears. Now, I thought, we have to play with the *terminal* ball and hope for the best.

During the beginnings of Kelly's health crisis, I missed the fairies who had once visited our house every night.

After Alan's accident, when Kelly was eight, she saw a movie in which two little girls photographed fairies, and she conveniently ignored the ending of the film in which the fairy sightings turned out to be a hoax. That night before she went to bed, Kelly said she wanted to leave a note for the fairies, along with some food. Surprised, I went downstairs to fetch peanuts while she wrote a "howdy-do" letter to the little people. We turned over a cardboard box as a makeshift altar and left a bowl of peanuts and the note on top of it. She went to bed and I went back to writing and forgot all about it. The next morning Kelly was in tears that the fairies hadn't responded, and I cursed myself for falling asleep without even thinking about writing a reply.

"It's because it was the wrong food," I said quickly. "Fairies like sweet things. We should have known that." And so, the next night we left M&Ms in the bowl, and that was when the fairies started to talk back. Every night Kelly left notes about her school day and questions about life in general. "Is my daddy ever going to get better?" she wrote one time, and the fairy queen, Mab, said that he definitely would, although being hit in the head always made someone a bit different. The fairies often left little photographs or portraits of themselves and a fairy "roll call," giving all their names, mostly based on flowers—Cornflower, Daisy, Violet, Comfrey, Chamomile. There was one fairy Kelly really loved, Nimby, who was the bad-boy fairy. He was always trying to steal babies or take food when he wasn't supposed to. Mab told Kelly all about him, and one night Nimby left a brief note himself. The notes, with very tiny handwriting, were on parchment paper ripped into tiny pieces.

Even though I was staying up until three or four in the morning to write the notes, I believed in them, too. I believed it when the fairies said they were everywhere, and not just in England, and that they were always watching out for us. Nimby told us how many fairies we nearly stepped on just when we took our dog out for a walk in the park. He had a lot of funny stories about hitching rides on dogs and also about playing tricks on other fairies, especially on Mab, whose authority he liked to flout.

I thought a lot about the fairies when we were at Children's Hospital, wondering if I could bring them back and have them fly around the corridors and make us laugh and give us hope. Kelly had always been so much fun as a kid, in her ability to believe. I don't want to call it gullibility. She just enjoyed fanciful stories of how the world was put together, and if she saw a character on television or in a movie, she believed she could make contact with it. When she was three she became obsessed with an old movie played on the Disney Channel, *The Wilderness Family*, about a hippie couple and their kids who move to the Rocky Mountains to live with raccoons and bears.

"I want to write them a letter," she said, and dictated a note asking if she could come live with them. She wanted to bring along Cosmo, our cat. She waited for two weeks every day at the mailbox until I finally got it through my head that she wasn't going to forget. The next day, their response appeared, and I was glad that she didn't notice that the stamp hadn't been cancelled.

She was excited but then disappointed, because although all four members of the family, even the little girl and boy, had included cool notes to her, the dad had to tell her the bad news that she'd have to wait to visit. They didn't have enough wood or food for another person, and they were afraid that their pet bear might eat Cosmo.

Then came the many letters to Big Bird asking if she could visit Sesame Street. He was a little less satisfying as a correspondent—he sent back a color postcard of himself on the fly because he was traveling everywhere and just didn't have the time or place to host her. It was a good picture and a thoughtful message, but still the Big Bird fixation lasted for a lot less time than her affection for the Wilderness Family.

"Remember the little men with the daggers?" she asked me once during the year of hospitalizations.

"Oh yeah," I said, smiling about another one of my parental deceptions. Kelly'd had strep throat when she was four, and as I've mentioned, she'd never even taken antibiotics before that. So there she was, a medicine virgin, suddenly faced with swallowing what seemed like massive amounts of yucky pink liquid.

"You gotta take it, Kelly, or you won't get better," I pleaded.

"No. It tastes terrible." (She still couldn't say her *l*'s or her *r*'s, so it sounded more like "tewwible." The antibiotic liquid was tewwible, and she saw "awwigators" in the Schuylkill River.)

"Yeah, but do you know what's in the medicine?" I asked.

Kelly looked at me quizzically.

"Little guys with daggers. They live in the pink stuff, and once they go down your throat, they jump out and they kill all the bad guys. That's why you feel some stabbing right now, because the bad guys are down there stabbing at *you*, and now you gotta send the other guys with the daggers to get them. They're bad guys, germs, and they need someone to *kill* them."

The story worked, somewhat. But it would take more than three swallows for her to get the stuff down, and then I would have to jump around karate-chopping the air and making the appropriate sound effects. It was a lot of work for each dosage, but worth it once the strep throat started to go away and her fever started descending. But Kelly was relentless with wanting stories, so the bad guys with daggers had to be done exactly the same way each time, and with great fanfare. I was often sabotaging myself that way as a parent, inventing fun strategies that backfired because they had to get more and more elaborate.

Take the shoe struggle, for instance. Between when she started to walk and when she was, say, ten, Kelly *hated* wearing shoes, and getting them onto her feet each morning was always a struggle. Following the advice from child-rearing books, I tried to involve her in the fun parts of footwear—if I gave my child a choice of which shoes to put on, the books said, she would feel more in control and despise footwear less. So I invented a pompous French shoe salesman who each day sat her down and tried to "sell" her various models. Putting on my best Pepé Le Pew accent, I would raid her closet, showing her socks with cartoon characters and various sneaker and patent leather models. It was fun, the first five or six times. But Kelly dragged it out until the French shoe salesman became downright irate and then threatened to quit altogether. He was an unhappy character in our house for a year after that, a slave to his trade. The only household employee who had it worse was Madame Snack Tray Purveyor, another ill-conceived character who tried to control Kelly's rampant snacking by limiting her choices to a well-balanced snack tray that Madame would carry from the kitchen to Kelly's bedroom each night. At first the snack tray purveyor attacked her subject with gusto, describing the graham crackers, Crazy Cow tinfoil squares, apple slices, and tiny yogurt samples with verve and dedication. Why, her tray was a veritable paradise of tiny snacks! But after only a few days on the job, Madame Snack wearied of her task and began arguing with the client. Within a week, the purveyor detested the very idea of a snack tray. What had she been thinking, to attempt this sort of product placement?

At the hospital, opportunities for creative coercion were more limited as I tried to cajole the preadolescent Kelly to drink more water or submit to various examinations. It was sad to watch her as we wended our way through the Children's Hospital system, since there was no longer any magic that would disguise the reality of being pricked and prodded all day long.

The child who had been terrified of needles, for example, quickly became the weary consumer, offering up her wrists and arms to be pricked again and again. After the first few weeks, she hardly noticed the wide variance in skill between phlebotomists—if it hurt, she just grasped my arm silently or squeezed her eyelids tight while tiny tears escaped from under her lashes.

"She's good," one lab nurse said after Kelly had had blood drawn for probably the thirtieth time.

"That was nothing," Kelly said. "What was it? Nine vials? My record is fourteen!"

At times like that, I realized that the fairies had left our lives long ago. I hoped that they were zipping around the hospital on some other ward, leaving notes for younger kids who needed them.

3. Hurry Up and Wait

A hospital bed is a parked taxi with the meter running.

Groucho Marx

The next afternoon, they did the liver biopsy. It was a long wait—why, I wondered, did they make kids wait so long in a hospital designed to cater to children. Kelly wasn't allowed to eat for the entire morning and early afternoon.

She was not completely under during the procedure, even though she wasn't supposed to sense anything.

"Mom, I could feel it," she said, crying only a half hour later in the recovery room. "I felt them go in and, like, snip it." Her chest was heaving with sobs.

"Now, honey, you rest," the recovery room nurse said. "She's a feisty one." She turned to me and rolled her eyes. "They're usually still asleep."

The nurse had told me that Kelly wouldn't remember the biopsy, but she was very wrong. They'd used a drug, Versed, that wasn't very effective as a sedative for Kelly. She didn't stop crying after the procedure, and by the time they were wheeling her back to her room, she had descended into hysteria.

Poor Kelly. Doctors and nurses never believe it, but she's nearly impossible to sedate, and she seems to develop allergies to drugs that rarely affect others. The night before, the doctors put her on fresh frozen plasma because the clotting factor in her own blood had been so compromised. The doctor explained they had to protect against the possibility that she might bleed out during the biopsy. But in the middle of the night they'd had to add Benadryl, an antihistamine, to her intravenous drip because she had started itching from the plasma. It's rare, it turns out, for a person to be allergic to blood products, but Kelly is. Yet until her blood could once again clot normally, they had to give her plasma, especially on the eve of a liver biopsy, when even the small puncture wound could be risky. (Kelly was also put on massive amounts of vitamin K, something lacking in all patients with serious liver problems. It's vitamin K that helps us all stop bleeding when we are cut or bruised.)

When we got to her room we realized that something bad must have come back on her roommate's tests, because our stuff had been evacuated and whisked away to a large room at the end of the corridor, a kind of graveyard for old monitoring equipment. When I demanded to know what was happening, our nurse just said that there had been a room shift. I later was told that no one knew why Kelly's eight-year-old roommate and her brother were so sick, and although they were exploring possible toxins near their house, they were also wondering if an infectious strain of some new hepatitis had felled them. I'm glad I hadn't known about the possibility of contagion the night before the biopsy, or my anxiety levels would have been even worse.

An hour after Kelly was settled into her new room, she still couldn't stop sobbing or thrashing around.

"Hmm," said the nurse who had just come on duty. "This is a fairly typical reaction for a teenage girl."

"What do you mean?" I said.

"I mean that this drug, Versed, does this to preadolescent girls. They get really weepy."

"Then why do you use it?"

"Because it's a good drug!"

"But it can't be a good drug if a patient has an adverse reaction," I said, proud of myself for using the medical jargon.

"We always use it," said the nurse, sorry by now that she'd opened up a can of worms.

Weepy is one thing; hysterical is another. What concerned me most was the rash that was spreading all over Kelly's body, and that she couldn't seem to get enough air in her lungs. No matter how much my mother and I tried to calm her, we couldn't get her to stop panting. I asked the nurse to get a doctor for us. Then, almost forty minutes later, I *demanded* that she get a doctor.

My mother is always uncomfortable when I show any signs of confrontation with medical staff, but she often talks about that night as a good illustration of why a patient has to speak up.

"If you hadn't *insisted* that they get you a doctor, poor Kelly would have kept suffering for hours," she's said to me more than once. That night my mom stood over her granddaughter hoping that by stroking her head or rubbing her legs she could somehow will her into taking full breaths and calming down. Only extra Benadryl did the trick, and its soporific effect finally knocked Kelly out and carried her away from the realm of the invasive liver biopsy and into sleep.

I liked the doctor who showed up—he hadn't performed the biopsy, but he was one of the kinder gastroenterologists we met at the hospital and he just happened to be on call that night.

"Yep, that's a pretty classic allergy," he said, taking note of the erupting rash and shallow breathing. I didn't realize it, but from that moment on, the doctors I had at CHOP never believed me when I told them Kelly was allergic to the sedative. The allergy to Versed would show up again at one of Kelly's other hospital stays, even though I always informed medical personnel of the problem. Later, at the Mayo Clinic, one doctor confirmed that although it's rare, patients can develop a serious allergy to the drug. I felt vindicated.

But now, with this newest dose of Benadryl dripping into Kelly's veins, the trauma was over and we were ready to face what we would find out from the biopsy. (Ah, how many times Benadryl saved us—even its inventor took one every night, as a sleeping pill—becoming an easy, non-narcotic way to get Kelly to settle down and, to me at least, a kind of miracle drug in those first few months of her illness.)

As organs go, the liver suffers from public relations problems. It's just not a sexy thing, like the heart or lungs or brain. It's big and gloppy, and most people are insecure in what they know about it. I know I was. When Kelly got sick, I'd been writing about health issues a lot, and especially about the brain. For the writer and the reader, the brain is kind of fun and kicky—like a pet puppy—whereas the liver is like, well, a lump of wet newspaper. No personality whatsoever. You hardly ever see an anthropomorphic cartoon featuring the liver, for example, whereas you'll often see stylized cartoons of the heart or lungs or brain.

There are other reasons we don't respond warmly to stories about human livers. For one thing, we *eat* the livers of other animals more often than we do other organs. Many of us know what chopped liver tastes like, even if it's from a calf or a chicken. How many of us know what lung or heart tastes like?

The liver's job is unglamorous, too. It is not part of the higher portions of our existence; we don't breathe or think with it. We filter with it: It's kind of the garbage man of organs, taking out the bad stuff before the rest of the waste gets sent to the small and large intestines and eventually to the colon. The liver is not a lofty organ. It's "down there," doing its work alongside the pancreas and kidneys and intestines. The liver gets a kind of a bum rap just by its association with bad stuff, too—the drugs we take, legal and illegal, are filtered by the liver, and then, of course, there's alcohol, which we humans invented as soon as we could and which our livers are tasked to remove as well as they can. Cirrhosis (or hardening) of the liver, which can occur with many diseases and conditions, is most often associated with heavy drinking, and so even talking about it raises suspicions. Those of us who drink try not to think of the liver, because it's hard to imagine what the booze is doing to it. The liver doesn't "cough" like the lungs. We can take a drag of smoke and pretty much feel what it is doing to our lung tissue, but a few glasses of wine pass silently through our big fleshy sentinels.

Even the word for liver inflammation, *hepatitis*, has bad connotations. I learned early on not to tell most people the real name of Kelly's disease, autoimmune hepatitis, because they would often physically move away from me as I said it. The general public doesn't understand that *hepatitis* merely means inflammation. They think it means bad things, such as contagion and death. The word *hepatitis* evidently reeks of dirty needles and unprotected sex. Even the highly educated principal of Kelly's private school initially thought my daughter was contagious when I said she had autoimmune hepatitis. Since the early days, I've spoken to many others with AIH, and we all agreed that it's much easier to tell people that you're suffering from a rare autoimmune disease that destroys the liver.

When I found out my kid's organ was in stage four of disintegration, I had to take a crash course in Liver 101. Since then, I've often found myself wanting to sign on as some sort of daft PR agent for our lowliest organ. Watching Kelly almost felled by organ failure, I gained new respect for the liver itself and for how resilient it is. It's no surprise that it was one of the first organs successfully transplanted, and it's absolutely amazing that physicians can now do transplants from live donors using only half the liver. If I took any comfort at all from AIH almost destroying Kelly's liver, it was in finding out about the organ's amazing powers. Unlike the heart or kidneys or lungs, the liver *can* regenerate, and at a remarkable rate. While Kelly's condition could have been a death sentence, and would have been a hundred years ago, now that the doctors were bombarding her liver with anti-inflammatory drugs, she had a very good chance of regaining normal function.

In the Middle Ages, the liver and gall bladder were associated with anger, with the "bile" a person could taste—the bitter acid of anger. An overactive liver meant rage. The Chinese still see the liver meridian as governing the emotions in many ways, and when I was in the midst of raging premenstrual syndrome (PMS) in my thirties, I endured a lot of acupuncture treatments by practitioners who explained to me that my liver meridian governed the mood swings and physical discomfort I was experiencing monthly.

If I were to design a PR campaign for the human liver, I think I would refer back to the olden days, when the liver ruled equally with the heart and mind, back to a time when good digestion meant a peaceful soul. One account I read about the liver said that it is often thought of as a "stoic" organ; it rarely complains, until it has been totally abused. Nowadays, it seems that we neglect the liver or at least rarely think of it, until something goes wrong.

And now the doctors at CHOP had put a needle into Kelly's liver and extracted a small tissue sample to see what was going on in there. I had worked on a museum exhibit about coal mining and seen the core samples, long tubes of ore brought up by hollow drills from the center of the mines. So this was the image I had: A small core of Kelly's liver would be extracted and examined. The blood tests, so far, had told us that her liver was damaged, that it was desperately straining to do its job. The elevated test numbers meant that it couldn't work efficiently while being attacked by the t-cells, and now the biopsy would tell the doctors more of the story. Specifically, they were looking for smooth antibodies and other signals of distress, and for telltale signs of cirrhosis. The liver biopsy is the major tool used by physicians to "stage" liver disease, meaning that they can tell by the quality of the tissue samples just how damaged the organ is. There are five stages of liver disease, with five being closest to complete failure. It was through the biopsy that we learned that Kelly's liver, while putting on a valiant struggle in the last year, was now in stage four. Antibodies had been bombarding it, changing its texture and forcing it to harden and lose its effectiveness as the body's main filter.

When I look back, that first hospitalization (out of a total of five) was the most satisfying. We had the illusion that things were getting done, problems solved. Little did we know that there would be no definitive solutions.

Kelly, it was determined, had classic autoimmune hepatitis type 1. We should be happy, Dr. Palmer said, that one of the hallmarks of the disease was how well it responded to anti-inflammatory drugs such as steroids (most commonly prednisone) and to Imuran (azathioprine), an immunosuppressant drug. That's the standard treatment in the beginning: a big wallop of prednisone combined in a kind of cocktail dosage with Imuran, and sometimes Ursodiol, or ursodeoxycholic acid, a compound the Chinese discovered in the livers of black bears (hence the root word *urso*). Oddly enough, doctors cannot determine how accurate a diagnosis of AIH is until they see how well a patient responds to treatment. The better Kelly responded to the drugs, the more likely it would be that she actually had the disease. This seemed like a catch-22 to me. I had never heard of a disease in which the response to the drug proves its diagnosis. Yet, again and again in my research on AIH, I've seen response to drug treatment listed as part of the diagnosis.

A year and a half later we got to meet the very man who had "discovered" and named autoimmune hepatitis type 1 in the 1970s, Dr. Albert Czaja, who practices at the Mayo Clinic in Minnesota. He's a great guy and I loved having him weigh in on Kelly's condition. But actually meeting a man who had discovered and named a disease made me wonder if it's worse to die from something that's never been named or something that has been codified. Nowadays we can't stand the unknown, so it's almost unthinkable that people died of a disease we never knew existed. Thousands must have died of AIH without anyone knowing what it was. Identifying, codifying, and studying diseases are all steps toward a cure, I suppose. The most interesting thing I ever heard from a doctor about this topic was also at the Mayo Clinic, when I was musing aloud about why no one I'd met had ever heard of Kelly's disease.

"Simple," the doctor, a kidney specialist, said, "because no celebrity has ever had it or talked about it."

In America, even diseases must have personalities—when someone such as Christopher Reeve has a spinal condition, then we want to know more about it. When Michael J. Fox develops Parkinson's, we want to read about it. I'm at the right age to remember how much Betty Ford and Happy Rockefeller did for breast cancer. It seems that no one ever felt comfortable talking about it until one of the goddesses of celebritydom stepped down from above to say that they'd contracted the illness. Someday a celebrity *will* get AIH and make it sexier. Maybe, too, someday AIH and other autoimmune liver diseases will be cured definitively, which will also make them more appealing to the general public. Right now AIH is incurable—the patient's best hope is to go into remission, which can happen for months or years at a time but almost never lasts. The recurrence rate is 80 percent.

AIH is relatively rare—in 1996, there were 1,156 cases in the United States. That means that it strikes only 1 in 235,294 people. Of course, that doesn't count the number of cases that go undiagnosed. It's also much rarer in children. The average person with AIH type 1 is a woman, age twenty-five to forty-five. It also seems to follow the pattern of many other autoimmune diseases in that it strikes in Western and Northern European communities. The cutting-edge specialists in the United States are at the Mayo Clinic, but in Europe it is in London and Frankfurt where the most studies are conducted.

In the end, does it matter how you got something, or why? Does it matter that others have it? You just want it out of you. The notion that a hidden enemy had been destroying one of my daughter's organs was unbearable. I wanted the disease nuked out, and that's pretty much what happened next. Kelly began her drug treatments replete with all the terrible side effects, and we began our new lives of knowing that we'd saved our daughter from something terrible we hadn't even known was happening to her.

Like so many great experiments, the one to save Kelly started with a big mistake. Our pharmacy misread the doctor's instructions—or maybe they were unclear—for Kelly's prednisone dosage. The pills were twenty milligrams apiece, and Kelly was supposed to take three a day. Instead, the instructions said to take one per day. Prednisone is a very strong steroid medicine, so even twenty milligrams a day is a lot. People with asthma or arthritis and patients on chemotherapy, who need prednisone to help fight off swelling, will often take twenty as the highest dosage possible.

Things were great when Kelly was only on a twenty-milligram dose because she didn't start feeling the extreme side effects prednisone can cause. I didn't know she was taking the wrong dosage, and I couldn't suspect how much upping the dose a few weeks later would wreak havoc with her body. In the first three weeks after she got out of the hospital, things seemed to be sailing along just fine. Gee, if this is the worst it's going to get, then it's not that bad, I thought to myself. Famous last words.

A writer is supposed to analyze how she feels about the characters in her books, so let me come clean here. Prednisone became a major character in Kelly's story, and even though I should be grateful to

Prednisone for saving my daughter's life, I hate "him." One of my friends, who writes for pharmaceutical companies, told me about a focus group study a big company did with consumers about antibiotics. The researchers created personalities for different antibiotics. Augmentin was the proud old grandpa, the venerable head of the antibiotic family, who was always reliable and trustworthy but a little old-fashioned. His wife, Tetracycline, was flighty and emotional, but effective. Their grandchildren included Cipro, a feisty young man who could go in and immediately control the situation.

These people are crazy, I thought as my friend described the narratives the pharmaceutical ad men had created. But the point was to get people to talk about their allegiances to the drugs and, specifically, to see if they would accept more newfangled antibiotics if the researchers presented them in a positive light.

I've given a lot of thought to prednisone's personality and why I hate him so much. Prednisone is a bully, but he's not the sort of bully you can pick out right away. He's the type of bully who flatters and cajoles you into thinking he is the best friend you'll ever have. Prednisone promises things: He'll get rid of your symptoms and make your blood tests successful. He'll make you, at first, full of energy. Your first encounters with prednisone, at any dose, will make you feel so much better immediately that you'll suspend your worries about what happens next.

I'd like to say that prednisone is the Dr. Faustus of drugs, but that is a bit too dignified a description. The drug is more comically diabolical, like Rumpelstiltskin, promising to spin straw into gold in exchange for, instead of your first born, a few pounds of flesh. Most people who make deals with prednisone regret it a lot afterward. I've also heard people say that treating someone with prednisone is a bit like aiming a cannon at a barn door. It's not a subtle drug; it will just bombard any inflammation until it starts to shrink. And then, about the time you are starting to bask in all the good it is doing for you, prednisone gives you its one-two bully punch. Sure, it's working to fight off your disease, but it's also working to give you bloat, blur your vision, rot your bones, and make you sleepless, insane, and fat as a pig. Sure, your liver is getting better, or you've stopped wheezing from your asthma, but now you have to worry about why your face is as round and almost as big as the moon, and why hair is growing on weird parts of your body, and why you suddenly look like the Hunchback of Notre Dame.

Prednisone has a romantic history. It was first used at the Mayo Clinic in 1948 to treat severely arthritic patients. Within days of starting the drug, people who couldn't walk or lift even a teacup suddenly moved without pain for the first time in years. It must have seemed like a miracle, just as dopamine did for that first generation of Parkinson's patients. The story of dopamine treatment for Parkinson's was beautifully told by Dr. Oliver Sacks in his book *Awakenings.* The Parkinson's patients, some of whom had been "frozen" for years, unable to move or speak, suddenly "woke up" when dosed with dopamine. They resumed their lives, only to find that, after a while, the drug had many bad side effects and even began to be inadequate. Just as with dopamine, it always takes a few months for prednisone's serious side effects to show up.

How does prednisone work? No one really knows for sure, except that it is the synthetic version of cortisol, the hormone naturally produced by the body to help our metabolism and aid us in coping with stress. Prednisone is a corticosteroid, a class of hormones that are regulators in the body. Unfortunately, when an artificial version of a natural steroid is administered, the body is not able to handle it well. Normal adrenal function closes down, and the artificial cortisol wreaks havoc with metabolism and bone maintenance and production. In effect, the prednisone *becomes* the patient's only adrenal system.

So, in those first few weeks, Kelly was like a time bomb about to go off. From talking to friends who are doctors, I learned that the highest dosage of prednisone a person normally can take without any side effects is five milligrams, so even at twenty milligrams, she was at risk of having some serious side effects. But twenty milligrams didn't seem to affect her, except to start to reduce her liver numbers (meaning the inflammation was going down) and give her a nice sense of energy. During those first weeks with Kelly on the lower dose of prednisone, we were lulled into thinking that the drugs would do nothing but help her.

Two weeks after the first hospital visit we went in for her first blood test, and two days later Dr. Palmer called to ask what, exactly, Kelly had been taking. She wanted me to hold the bottles in my hand and tell her *exactly* what had passed Kelly's lips each day.

I told her the Imuran dosage and then the Urso numbers. Then we got to the prednisone bottle, and I told her it was twenty milligrams.

"Three times a day, right?"

"No. Once. It says once."

"That's wrong. That dose is wrong. Kelly was supposed to take three a day. It's supposed to be sixty milligrams."

"Well, she hasn't. It says here, 'once a day.' "

"I *knew* it," Dr. Palmer said. Evidently Kelly's liver numbers, the ones that indicated severe inflammation, were starting to descend—her ALT and AST numbers had already dropped by a few hundred—but

Dr. Palmer said that they should have gone down even more with a larger prednisone dosage, the one she had prescribed.

I wish I'd known then that this was a defining moment, the moment when my kid's treatment would shift into hellish gear. Under Dr. Palmer's instructions, I started dosing Kelly three times a day with the prednisone. It wasn't easy. Kelly acted as if I were trying to poison her. It turned out that I was, since as soon as she starting getting another forty milligrams of prednisone a day, all the bad side effects appeared.

This was in the beginning of April. By mid-May, with Kelly taking the full dose of prednisone for two months now, she had blown up in front of my eyes, gaining eighty pounds in six weeks. She'd sprouted hair all over her upper lip and on her cheeks. Her beautiful green eyes had sunk into her face, eclipsed by huge moonlike cheeks that distorted the lower part of her face. And then there was the coup de grace: a definitive "hunchback" at the nape of her neck, an ugly protuberance that sprouted wiry hairs. As if all of these ugly features weren't enough, she developed patches of strange beadlike acne all over her face and upper arms.

Ever since Kelly's diagnosis, my financial situation, which had been precarious to begin with, had gotten worse by the week. Even when Alan was sick, I had managed to finish a few of my projects, but now, five years later and with another loved one whose health was in peril, I ended up dropping out of several lucrative museum contracts (I had developed a sideline of writing the captions for exhibits), and all I had left was one commitment to write a college graduation speech for a famous shoe magnate.

Basically Kelly and I were living on maxed-out credit cards, until I started borrowing copiously from my mother. (Kelly made a game out of the credit-card problem, creating a little ditty called "Living on the Edge," which she liked to sing or hum under her breath as we waited in a checkout line to see if a particular credit card would go through. She was in that preadolescent phase in which minor poverty seemed glamorous.) Over the year that she was sick and hospitalized five times, I managed to earn a whopping nine thousand dollars, about a tenth of the earnings of my most lucrative years as a freelance writer (although I'm just being vain, because there were many years when I earned far less, but never as little as nine thousand bucks). And just at a time when I couldn't concentrate enough to work or hustle to get new assignments, our expenses were rising: the pills, new clothing, camp tuition. Summer was coming, and Kelly now faced the nightmare of trying to fit into any teenager clothing after gaining eighty pounds.

Kelly finished the school year in a kind of race with ugliness. She couldn't get out of the seventh grade fast enough, and of course no one understood what was happening to her appearance. Her body, distorted with the new weight, had developed stretch marks and sores. Her breasts, which had been developing at a moderate rate, were now huge and pendulous, and one of them had stretched into a strange straight shape and hung nearly to her waist. In February, when she was diagnosed with her illness, she had weighed 119 pounds. By June, she weighed 190.

I dreaded the inevitable chore of buying a bathing suit for her summer months at home and away at camp. Even though I had started having severe financial problems, I decided to take her to the fanciest shop in Philadelphia, which specialized in cruisewear and designer suits. It was the only thing I could think of—perhaps an expensive suit would help camouflage what the bathing suit industry euphemistically calls "figure flaws."

What a disaster. With every suit, Kelly hated herself more. She stood behind the curtain, at first cowering and then later crying without letup. A young salesgirl tried her best, bringing in the most modest one-pieces the store had to offer. At one point, as Kelly tried on yet another impossible candidate, I took the salesgirl aside and whispered. "My daughter has had a very serious illness. She almost died, and the drugs are making her gain impossible amounts of weight."

I immediately regretted saying it. At first it flustered the shopgirl, and then made her too attentive. Still, I had to say something. I couldn't stand the idea that she thought my kid was either (a) fat and ugly and looked like hell in every suit; or (b) a little princess who couldn't be satisfied with anything.

So what does that say about me? Why did I even care about what the salesgirl thought? I only wanted Kelly to be happy, and of course in the midst of our shopping experience I realized that buying a bathing suit was not going to come close to making that happen. In the end we paid too much for an aquamarine Calvin Klein that did nothing for Kelly's body, but at least it covered up her stretch marks and didn't reveal too much of her newly fleshy upper arms.

It was only years later—this year, in fact—that I got my own visit from Mr. Prednisone himself and found out firsthand what it feels like to live in a steroidized body. It's funny, because you would think I'd have been savvy about it, but prednisone ambushed me just as surely as he ambushed my baby girl. After a series of failed back operations, I found a surgeon who was willing to go in and fix what was wrong, but only if I submitted to some diagnostic spinal blocks. The idea was that if my back responded to the blocks, then the surgeon would have a better idea exactly where my problem was and what he had to do when he opened up my spine.

Well, the chemicals in the block are made up primarily of prednisone. The first shot made me feel great. The pain down there was gone, and I could stay up for hours writing and reading and even cleaning up the house. When that wore off, I got the second shot, and that was when everything went crazy. I called friends to scream at them. I erupted at any little thing Kelly did. I was ravenously hungry. I was weepy. The pleasant bursts of energy turned into fits of insomnia. And then I started to blow up like the Michelin man. As soon as I noticed this happening, I curtailed my calories to a great extent. Still, it seemed as if I were gaining at least five pounds a day. I told East Coast friends on the phone, friends who hadn't seen me for six months, that I was getting enormous, but they didn't believe me. And then, when I finally got up the nerve to weigh myself, I was shocked to see that I weighed a hundred pounds more than I did that time last year. Even accounting for two other pain medications I'd taken that cause weight gain, it still meant that I'd gained over fifty pounds in two short months. Worse was my face: There were no visible cheekbones at all. My vision was actually obscured by the giant mounds of flesh that had arisen under each eye. It was official: I was no longer human. I was an enormous homunculus, part human, part steroid.

I had my experience with prednisone when I was over fifty years old, after many other experiences in which I saw my body "betray" me, or at least surprise me. I'd been through the rigors and changes of pregnancy, for example. But poor Kelly had no context. All she knew was that she was supposedly sick and had to take pills that were making her look scary to other kids. A rumor started around the school that Kelly was dying. Thankfully, school ended and she could escape growing larger and more ungainly in a daily observation tank.

Long after Dr. Palmer insisted on that high dosage of prednisone, I learned that many doctors never prescribe more than twenty milligrams of the drug to children, and never for more than a few weeks. Perhaps if we had kept on course with the single pill per day, Kelly's liver enzymes would have settled down, although it would have taken longer. But resolution of a flare-up of a chronic disease is not a race, so why did my kid have to suffer? Then again, maybe the massive doses of the drug in the beginning are what propelled her into remission.

A few weeks after Kelly was discharged from the hospital, and about the time Dr. Palmer increased her drug dosage, she and I were headed down the street to fetch a DVD from the local "cool" video house, the one with all the foreign and independent films, when we ran into Stephen Fried, my former editor at *Philadelphia* magazine and a longtime writer friend. I was surprised at what I blurted out after Stephen innocently asked me how we were.

"Kelly's been diagnosed with a terrible liver disease, and we were in Children's Hospital, and now we're taking it easy."

Stephen's first instinct was journalistic. He looked Kelly up and down nervously. "Liver, huh? Do you know Andrew Corsello? Used to write here in Philly, then went to *GQ*. His liver failed while he was here. He almost died. Yeah, you should call him and say I told you to. Andrew wrote this whole thing about his liver failure. He knows everything about the liver."

"Oh my God. How old was he?"

"When it happened?" Stephen said. "Oh, he was in his twenties. Call him."

I looked over at Kelly, who had turned red as a beet while we were talking. Red is good, I thought. She's not pale, and that's a good sign.

I called Andrew the next day at his magazine; it took him a few more days to get back to me. It was nice of him to respond, because how many people want to talk about something once they're cured of it? (I was already beginning to suspect that one did not recover easily from a brush with autoimmune liver disease. When I asked Dr. Palmer and one of her assistants if they could locate a patient in remission who would talk to Kelly, they said they'd found two of them, but neither wanted to relive the experience by talking to a current patient.)

Andrew's story was very curious. He'd been hiking with his fam ily, carrying his four-year-old stepsister on his back, and when he returned from the hike, he felt unusually tired. By the next day, his liver had failed to the point where his doctor father chartered a jet to take him to Pittsburgh should he be able to get a liver transplant. Andrew never flew to Pittsburgh. Instead, a barrage of doctors began pumping him with steroids, saving his life. Later, he went on to the same type of drug regimen as Kelly, including a very high dose of prednisone. He remembered the side effects all too well.

"Does she have the rage?" he asked. Andrew, a tall guy of over two hundred pounds, had been on eighty milligrams of prednisone a day. He said he couldn't believe that anyone would give a child sixty milligrams.

"I remember throwing dishes against the wall for no reason," he said. "One time I saw a guy toss a candy wrapper on the street in Manhattan, and I had to turn around and walk away so that I wouldn't pummel him to death."

Andrew had had the weight gain from the steroids, too, and the general weakness. Before his liver incident, he'd been a strong guy who lifted weights at the gym and played racquet sports. It took him several years, he said, to feel that strong again. He was philosophical about ever finding out exactly what had caused his liver to start consuming itself. He'd never even been officially diagnosed with AIH or any other liver illness.

"Livers are weird," he said, explaining that finding out just how fragile our livers are had scared him to death. "It's an organ that can just go haywire and destroy itself in a matter of days," he told me over the phone. "Once you get into the area of livers, you see all sorts of mysteries. And I don't trust anything I eat anymore. For example, I would watch it, if I were you, around all those dried mushroom products from China."

In some ways it was comforting to hear from Andrew. He was, after all, a liver disease survivor. But there was also something upsetting about how angry he still was about the fallibility of the organ. I guess no one who's been let down suddenly and forced to contemplate mortality in his twenties can be expected to be calm about it. I'll always be grateful that he raised a red flag about the sheer amount of prednisone Kelly was being given.

By the time Andrew and I made contact, Kelly *was* starting to climb the walls. A few weeks after Dr. Palmer upped her dosage to sixty milligrams, she came home from school crying.

"Neesa yelled at me, Mom." Neesa was Kelly's beloved art teacher, who had approached Alan and me asking permission to "groom" Kelly to get her into the local magnet school for the arts.

"I couldn't keep my hands from shaking and I kept wasting paper when I tried to cut things," Kelly explained. "Then I couldn't keep my hands from shaking when I tried to draw. I started laughing, and I guess she thought I was kidding around. I told her it was the medicine I was taking, and she said no medicine could make me so careless."

Neesa's reaction was totally understandable. I thought about calling her and telling her that drugs were indeed giving Kelly the shakes, but Kelly insisted that I not do so. She was too embarrassed, and in a few days school would be out anyway. But she was obviously upset that the drugs were now affecting her ability to do simple things. It was really the drugs, and not the disease, that caused her next hospitalization, but by that time she was out of school and we were well on our way into our Nightmare Summer.

4. The Body Rebels

> We admitted your patient, Kelly Crimmins, to the inpatient pediatric Gastroenterology Service in Philadelphia on May 31, 2001. This 12-year-old girl was admitted for a possible herpetic lesion, her autoimmune hepatitis, her renal hematuria, and her immunosuppression. She was placed on IV antibiotics and intravenous Acyclovir. The lesion did not progress. A biopsy of the lesion had been performed in Oakland and the results are still pending...

It was late May and my kid was three thousand miles away with her father, in trouble, and I didn't know it. I'd been traipsing around on a weekend getaway, with my cell phone uncharged as usual. I was a bad mom, I guess, because I just wasn't that worried about what Kelly was up to. Actually, I didn't want to be, and I was trying to will myself not to think about her AIH for just a few days. I was burned out from harassing her about her health, always making sure that she took the drugs I knew were beginning to disfigure her. After our daily morning fights to get the meds down her throat, I'd often sit on the living room couch and sob, wondering if I was doing the right thing bombarding her with toxins.

So now it was three months after her diagnosis and she was with her dad, attending her cousin's Bat Mitzvah in Oakland, California, and as soon as I dropped them off at the airport, I felt free. And I felt comfortable that Kelly would be surrounded by loving adult relatives.

But a few days later, Kelly got really sick. She and Alan had gone to a baseball game at Candlestick Park in San Francisco when she broke out into a terrible fever. When they got back to her aunt and uncle's house, her fever was 104. Then my sister-in-law noticed a large, red, nasty-looking sore, much like a canker sore but about ten times as big, on Kelly's shoulder and decided to take her to the emergency room at the Oakland Children's Hospital.

Opportunistic herpes. Blech. Evidently when patients take powerful immunosuppressants such as prednisone and Imuran in large doses, they can develop such sores because the body's normal defenses break down. So, just as a person might get a mouth sore because of being run down or on the brink of catching a cold, a "compromised" patient can also get such sores on other parts of the body. I remember reading about the prevalence of such lesions on HIV patients in the early days of the epidemic. They'd get run down and susceptible to many opportunistic infections.

The doctors at Oakland had a hard time believing that Kelly was sick with liver disease, because just three months after she'd begun treatment, the drugs had "nuked" the AIH out of her system. Her emergency blood tests came back normal, even her AST and ALT levels. Instead of the disease, now it was the drugs that were wreaking havoc with Kelly's fragile body. In one note on Kelly's hospital records, a doctor even wrote that he considered Kelly "in remission" from AIH. So they prescribed an antiviral drug to try to speed up the healing of the herpes sore (a version of the drug you see advertised in all those earnest genital herpes advertisements), and some ibuprofen to deal with her fever. Beyond that, there was nothing else they could do.

Alan finally reached me with the news of Kelly's emergency room visit in Oakland, and I talked to one of the Oakland doctors briefly. After consulting with Kelly's doctors in Philadelphia, it was determined that she should return as soon as possible so that they could see what was going on.

"With the levels of Kelly's medications, it's important that we hospitalize her to make sure she doesn't develop any further problems," Dr. Palmer told me when I contacted her by phone.

Poor Alan and Kelly. It was a hellish plane ride, with Kelly feverish and whiney, hanging all over Alan, even though by this time she weighed nearly more than he did. I met them at the airport in the evening and didn't like what I saw when Kelly stepped out of the security area. She looked paler than when she'd left, almost yellow, and when she walked, her arms and legs moved like a limp rag doll's. I couldn't wait to get her into her own bed, and Alan couldn't wait to get home himself and recharge. Seeing Kelly get so violently ill on his watch had been very difficult for him, and I took the opportunity once again to explain AIH to him and how serious it was.

Al's comprehension of her illness at the time was sketchy. I didn't understand the full extent of his inability to process the information until I got a call from our lawyer, Mark, who made a joke about Kelly's liver ailment, asking me if I was going to write a book about it and start calling Kelly "The Liver Princess." When I got very upset, Mark said he thought I wouldn't mind his joking about it since Al had said that what Kelly had was more like a bad flu and not very serious. As an alarm was going off in my head, I explained to Mark that what Kelly had could be fatal, developing a catch in my throat as I said it. (Damn that catch in my throat! I had to figure out how to talk about Kelly's illness without sounding pathetic, or crying, but it was hard.) I spent the rest of the conversation assuring Mark the lawyer that I didn't think he was a bad person for laughing about Kelly's illness. How could he tell what was going on with Alan leading the way?

I could only imagine what Kelly's shoulder sore had looked like when it was "fresh," because now it was hideous. I changed the bandage before she went to sleep and by morning it was inflamed and oozing. It almost looked like a flesh-eating wound.

That night, after getting Kelly to bed, I called Alan and tried to convey to him the seriousness of her illness. It was really bad timing; the poor guy was exhausted and stressed. I told him that what Kelly had was far more serious than the flu, and that many people can die of AIH if it goes undiagnosed. I could feel Alan's emotional pendulum begin to swing the other way. Now, instead of being cavalier, he was totally panicked—which was exactly what I didn't want to happen. That week I fielded several calls from friends and casual acquaintances saying that Alan had called to tell them that Kelly was *dying. Now.* Kelly, he said, *didn't have long to live.*

Was there no happy medium? Evidently not, for a man suffering from the side effects of a brain injury. Perhaps it was just too early in Alan's recovery for him to be able to see anything in less than black-and-white terms. Either Kelly was dying, or she wasn't. Either she had something a little worse than the common cold, or she had a terminal illness. I suppose I should have been more acclimated to the new, post-brain injury Alan by now, and especially to his limitations in reasoning and judgment, but Kelly's illness had caused a knee-jerk reaction in me: My kid was sick, and I wanted my old supportive husband back. I wanted someone who could understand the problem and talk to me about it. I wanted an ally in dealing with the doctors and not another child I had to "manage" during her illness.

Alan's problems with comprehension made me feel even more isolated. I worried about sharing good news with him, and about sharing my worst fears of losing our daughter, and I certainly couldn't discuss any of these nuances with Kelly. Yes, she had to know that she was seriously ill—and I confirmed this whenever she asked about it—but I couldn't share with her my doubts and fears the way I could with another adult. I had to protect her from my despair and confusion.

In the end, I had to accept that a complicated chronic condition such as autoimmune hepatitis (AIH) was simply outside Alan's comfort range emotionally and intellectually, but I still had to worry about Alan with regard to Kelly's doctors. Just as it was added stress for me to be the sole interpreter of the doctors' information and decisions, it was also added stress to have to worry about how Alan would come across to the health-care professionals treating Kelly. If he got frustrated or tired, he'd often lash out and begin to yell at them, at which point I'd have to take them aside to explain his condition. After all, I didn't want them to think we didn't want to hear about Kelly's illness, or appreciate what they were trying to do for her. But every time I tried to telegraph to the doctors that we were a "brain injury family," I worried that they would discriminate against us because of our problems. (Later, when we were shunted off to hospital psychiatrists because of Kelly's insomnia, this fear of mine came true—the psych interns constantly referred to our "family problems.")

The next day, after a restless night in her own bed, Kelly was once again admitted to the hospital via the emergency room. I had pleaded with Dr. Palmer to have Kelly admitted "normally," whatever that meant, but she'd said that without advance notice, her department didn't have any mechanism for a non-emergency admission. Kelly wasn't being admitted for a particular procedure, just for observation, so once again we had to go in through emergency. This seemed so stupid. Why couldn't a doctor just sign a form to allow one's child to get a hospital bed within, say, three hours, instead of the eight to eleven it took in the past? And once we were there again, why couldn't anyone dredge up the countless histories we'd already given to scores of interviewers? Why did we have to tell our story all over again?

In the emergency room, Kelly saw gastroenterologists and nephrologists. Her bladder seemed perpetually irritated, and she nearly always had a low-level bladder infection. It would be weeks before I'd find out that the high levels of prednisone were wreaking havoc on her kidneys, too. She also still peed blood frequently, and no one could tell us why.

Once Kelly got into a room, by late afternoon, we waited several more hours to see "real" doctors, but no one showed up until the next morning at six. Dr. Palmer was not on call the first few days, so we saw a team of nephrologists (kidney specialists—Kelly once again was displaying symptoms of a bladder infection) and gastroenterologists (liver and digestive specialists). I was beginning to get accustomed to the drill: Hordes of physicians would show up at unearthly hours to root you out of sleep and subject you to countless questions. At this point, the side effects of the prednisone were cropping up relentlessly, and after seeing how well Kelly had tolerated only twenty milligrams a day versus sixty, I began to wonder if we could drop her down to that dosage again. I didn't care if her liver numbers became normal more quickly at sixty milligrams; I just wanted her to go into remission without suffering so much. And now the California doctors *did* think she was in remission.

In Dr. Palmer's stead a kindly middle-aged male gastroenterologist, Dr. Blackburn, was attending, with an assistant I'd gotten along with in the past.

I asked to see them in the hallway and told the two of them that I'd watched the side effects from Kelly's prednisone and Imuran grow out of control. "The poor girl has gained eighty pounds," I said. "And she has stretch marks. And look at the acne; she didn't have that kind of acne a few weeks ago. Worse, look at that sore. She's run down. Her numbers were coming down before we escalated the dose. Can't we just go back to what she was taking?" I took a deep breath. "In fact, I *insist* that her prednisone dosage be lowered."

Dr. Blackburn patiently explained that we couldn't go back, but that we could start to wean her off the higher dose gradually, perhaps five milligrams every few days. This was the first I'd learned how important it was not to drastically change *any* dose of prednisone, because the drug shuts down normal adrenal activity almost completely, and it takes a while for that to start up again. I had to wonder why, then, we'd been able to *add* another forty milligrams of the stuff suddenly without worrying about side effects. Maybe reducing dosage is trickier than adding milligrams.

Dr. Blackburn really disappointed me. He seemed nice and concerned at first, but then I felt he began rationalizing, out loud, why Kelly had reacted badly to prednisone.

"Weight gain. Well, you know, she has that build, and as for the acne and the striations, well, she's fair, and so more prone to that sort of thing."

Five minutes after he walked out of the room with his assistant and team of students, I thought of everything I should have said to him. "What build? My kid was a hundred and nineteen pounds when this started! And what does being fair have to do with acne?" I was pretty certain he'd looked at me and thought, "Well, the Mother is overweight." Worse, I had seen his entire team nod gravely when he had said these things. It was the first time I'd seen a doctor rationalize spectacular side effects, but it wasn't going to be the last time, unfortunately.

Still, Dr. Blackburn was nice enough to start dropping Kelly's prednisone dosage. That decision lasted until the next day, when he walked in behind Dr. Palmer, his head lowered. Dr. Palmer was fuming. I could almost imagine the two of them, cartoon-like, with Dr. Palmer pulling Dr. Blackburn along by his ear and flinging him to the floor. Dr. Palmer was so angry that her face was bright red, and a vein in her forehead was throbbing.

"I don't know where you got the idea that Kelly's prednisone dosage could change," she said to me. She had one hand on her hip and her voice was quavering with anger as she took me aside and said: "Your daughter is still very sick. Her liver could flare up at any time, and her life could be seriously threatened. Is that what you want? You want to see Kelly back in the emergency room, with her liver failing?"

"I . . . I . . . I just think it's too much," I said. "I looked it up, and

I don't see any other child on that dose. Look at what it's done to her."

The Mother looks things up. I wish I hadn't put it that way, as if I had just casually surfed the Internet for random drug facts. And I wish I hadn't come on so strongly with Dr. Palmer on the very first day we met, telling her I wrote about medical issues. That was back when I thought of her as an ally. She had confided, that first day, that she knew well what it was like to have a child with a chronic illness, as one of her children had diabetes.

"Yes, she's had reactions," she said now. "But this is nothing compared to the AIH. I can't stress enough—we must keep her on these medications."

"For how long?"

"At least a year more."

A year? Kelly's system was already breaking down under the strain of these drugs. I'd sent my kid off to California and gotten her back with a high fever, an opportunistic sore, and the lowest energy level I'd seen yet. She shook all over and had trouble sleeping at night. How could she last another year on such high levels of prednisone? In all the reading I'd done, I hadn't found another case of juvenile AIH in which a kid stayed on that level of prednisone for more than six weeks. But I didn't say this aloud.

"I feel very strongly that Kelly shouldn't be on so much prednisone."

Dr. Palmer stared at me. "This boils down to trust," she said, "and I'm telling you what is best for your daughter. If that level of trust is not there, then maybe it is time for you to consider a second opinion."

She left abruptly, but not until she'd barked out orders to the bedraggled Dr. Blackburn. "I want the dosage to stay at sixty a day until further notice."

I had already considered a second opinion, or maybe Dr. Palmer had forgotten that I'd asked her, point blank, during one of Kelly's earliest appointments, where the best places to treat AIH were. "Right here at CHOP is one of them," she'd said. "I have about ten cases of kids sent here from all up and down the East Coast."

I remember calling my mom the very evening Dr. Palmer had told me that. I hadn't started out being dubious about Dr. Palmer and her crew—I was initially excited that we could get help for Kelly right at Children's Hospital. If Kelly had to have this horrible disease, I told my mom during that phone conversation, thank God one of the best places for treating it is right across the river from our house. I couldn't believe our good fortune. But as the weeks wore on and Kelly's side effects worsened, I began doing more active research on the best specialists for the disease. Again, and again, two places came up: in Rochester, Minnesota, and London, England. Dr. Albert Czaja, at the Mayo Clinic, and a married couple, Drs. Luigi and Vieri Muratori in London were highly recommended. I'd mentioned them to Kelly, and of course she'd wanted to go to London, since she and I had gone on a wonderful vacation there when she was ten. I knew, though, that I had to choose somewhere that would take our insurance, and chances were that the Mayo Clinic would.

I'd been holding back on calling the Mayo Clinic, partly because I was scared. My mother's friend Hansell had told us about a friend who decided to try the Mayo. It was one of the simplest things in the world, she said. You just call the Mayo Clinic and tell them you need help. They do the rest. On the day that Dr. Palmer insisted that Kelly remain on the high prednisone dose indefinitely, I was too chicken to go against her, but I never felt the same again about the level of care Kelly was getting at Children's Hospital. I wish now that I had challenged Dr. Palmer more, or that I had just decided to go with my instincts and lower the dose of prednisone, hoping to stave off the AIH. But at least the seeds of anger and mistrust had been planted, and the next day I got up the nerve to call the Mayo Clinic. I described Kelly's case in detail to the operator, and within minutes we had an appointment. But we had to wait more than two months, until the last days of August.

Kelly stayed in the hospital for another few days after Dr. Palmer's dictum about prednisone. More time on the mom cot for me, and more time watching Animal Planet and doing inane crafts projects for Kelly.

Then, a few days after we got home from the hospital, late one morning after I'd fed Kelly breakfast, the phone rang. It was Dr. Jones, the older kidney specialist who'd started us on our diagnostic journey at Children's Hospital. He had been away and wanted to catch up with us, he said.

"I was so sorry to hear that your daughter has AIH," he said. "Dr. Palmer is an excellent diagnostician, but I'm still sorry. I know your daughter will have to take drugs that will make it hard for her."

"Yes," I told him. "She's already having a lot of problems with the prednisone."

"Nasty stuff," the doctor said. "I had to take it for only a few days, for an inflammation. It made me crazy. I cleaned my house and garage from top to bottom. I couldn't stop moving, and I couldn't sleep. My wife didn't know what had gotten into me. I'm sorry your little girl has to take that."

The doctor was especially nice to have called me at home, but he'd said very little about Kelly's condition. In fact, he'd said more in the silences about Kelly's condition than when he addressed it directly. He was no longer on prednisone, so his experiences had become just a funny anecdote about a hyperactive version of himself. From what I was learning about AIH, Kelly might be on drugs like prednisone for the rest of her life. The side effects could become, eventually, a part of her and not just a bunch of funny stories. I was beginning to grasp the peculiar tragedy of chronic illness, which is that no one's minor or temporary experiences with similar pain or even similar medicines could compare with the daily grind of a lifelong sentence.

5. Romancing the Stone

> She was admitted to the service, medicated with Toradol, and maintained over a period of four or five days with good hydration. Despite this, she failed to pass stone fragments and suffered significant pain... We waited another 24 hours and therefore on Saturday morning, August 18, 2001, we went ahead and carried out a cystoscopy. We dilated the right ureter after a retrograde pyelogram confirmed some tiny calcul in the distal ureter. Once this was done, we were able to pass up an 8 French uteroscope and we were able to basket several small stones along the course of the distal third ureter. She had a significant amount of edema and swelling in the distal ureter that I think would have made passing these stones more difficult for her...
>
> *from a CHOP report*

As the long, hot summer muddled on, we tried our best to pretend that everything was normal for Kelly. The weight gain and other side effects of the drugs—a light coating of hair all over her now-rounded "moon" face, the hump on her back—began to seem more daunting, as the heat called for skimpier clothes.

That year Kelly had decided to go to sleepaway camp with her friend Maddy, who was fond of a primitive place in the Pine Barrens, an odd area only about an hour outside of Philadelphia. New Jersey-ites will proudly tell you that there are species of frogs and birds there found only in the Pine Barrens, but I can't say it's easy to pick them out. It's the part of New Jersey that millions of years ago was underwater; it's flat and sandy and underpopulated. Most folks think of it as the wasteland you must travel through to get to the ocean.

The Pine Barrens is a colorful place for folklore. The Jersey Devil, a strange hairy beast with many frightening tales attached, is from there, and some folklorists make it a specialty to study folktale variants from the region. It's believed that many of the Hessian soldiers who were conscripted to fight on the British side during the American Revolution ran away to the Pine Barrens and settled its sandy land. The place has two major products: mosquitoes and cranberries.

Back in the late winter, when Kelly was deciding to go to Girl Scout camp with Maddy, I hadn't given the facilities a second thought. It was primitive and cheap. By the time she'd gone through two hospitalizations, though, I began to worry a bit about how good it would be for her to go to a camp where most activities were physical, but after all she'd gone through, I hated to tell her she couldn't go away with her friend. I called the camp nurse and told her about Kelly's condition, and we dropped Kelly off with information about her autoimmune illness and the drugs she had to take at the nurse's office each day.

Poor Kelly didn't last long. It was one of the hottest summers on record, and the camp's only air conditioner was in the nurse's office. The kids had to go into the tepid peat-mossy lake several times a day to survive the heat. Plus, Kelly wasn't enthralled by camp culture, especially the campfires at Camp Wee-kee-weekinuddyit, as we called it. One revolved around the Native American's respect for wildlife, with elaborate stories about what would happen to chipmunks if they ingested chewing gum.

One Saturday, less than a week after Kelly had started camp, the Boyfriend and I were getting ready to go to a housewarming picnic when the phone rang. It was the nurse from Kelly's camp.

"Your daughter is in a lot of pain, and she has a very high fever," she said. She went on to say that she could get an ambulance for Kelly and have her taken to the local hospital, or did I want her to go to Children's Hospital instead?

I was in a panic. Part of me wanted Kelly to get immediate care, but realistically I knew that wouldn't happen in any hospital, not with the whole emergency room charade. I didn't think it was possible to cry so suddenly, but there I was, blubbering. It was back, the whole nightmare of the last few months. I needed comfort, but there was none to be had. I wondered what would have happened if we had left exactly on time and I hadn't gotten the phone call.

Instead of seeing what he could do to help, the Boyfriend decided to leave by himself for the barbecue. It was as if he couldn't get out of my house soon enough. He actually seemed angry that my inconsiderate child had ruined our date.

While I was getting things together, the phone rang again. It was my friend Frank Costello. Frank was my stand-up comedy partner and had worked with Alan at the courthouse years ago. He knew that Kelly was sick, but not the exact details.

"Frank! I can't talk. I have to go pick up my kid. She's really sick and I have to get her to the hospital."

I wish I had taken Frank up on his offer to rush over and go with me to the camp, but he lived more than forty minutes outside the city. Alan was away in Montana. I decided to go it alone—something I later regretted.

In the almost hour-long drive to the Pine Barrens, a complex thought did not cross my brain. It's a weird stop-and-go route, and I found myself concentrating to the point that my hands hurt from gripping the wheel of our small Toyota. Kid. Sick. Kid. Sick. Turn. Brake.

When I reached the turnoff for the camp's sandy driveway, I didn't find the charmingly bucolic spot where I'd dropped Kelly off the week before. Instead, I saw primitive conditions: tiny wooden huts crammed with kids' stuff, an uninviting buggy pond passing for a lake. This camp was cheap for a reason. Why had I put my kid into it at the one point in her life when she most needed modern conveniences? I couldn't even imagine her making the several-block-long hikes to the outhouses. By the time I got to the nurse's office I was beating myself up big time.

"Mom's here," the nurse said, leading me to a cot where a pale Kelly was languishing under a quilt. I sat down and felt her head. She was burning up.

"She's got a lot of pain—lower back—and she says she feels like she's going to throw up."

"Mommy, it feels like there's a bone down there."

"A bone?"

"A bone stabbing my vagina."

I looked up at the nurse. "Do you think it's a bladder infection?"

"Could be. Or kidneys. She should see a doctor, whatever it is," she said, handing me Kelly's medicine. She was relieved that Kelly was no longer going to be her problem, but very nice about it, too. We agreed that we would leave all of Kelly's other stuff in her cabin until we found out what was happening. I thought that would make Kelly feel less sickly, but really, at that point, I don't think she cared about being labeled as the sick kid. She just wanted to get out of there and out of pain.

Kelly lasted about three miles until the next waves of pain and nausea hit her. First she began screaming in a way I'd never heard her scream before. It wasn't a cry, and it wasn't a moan—it was a full-fledged nonverbal scream that sent chills up my spine. Then came the vomit. I pulled over to the side of the road and ran around to her door. She could barely stand up enough to get out, and with me tugging her, she stumbled on to the shoulder and fell to her knees puking. I didn't know when she'd last eaten, but nothing much was coming up, which made it even harder on her body—she almost seemed to be having convulsions, and it scared me.

Should I go back to the camp and call an ambulance? Was it going to be okay to keep driving? At this point I felt propelled toward Philadelphia, and I imagined the hassle it would be to reintroduce ourselves into the camp environment when they'd thought they were rid of us.

I clenched my teeth and told Kelly not to worry. She could scream or puke as much as she liked, but I was taking her to the hospital, to Children's, in the city, and we were going to go as fast as we could, so there was no sense in our stopping anymore.

And that's how I came to be driving down a New Jersey state highway with a yowling kid puking out the window. It was the longest short drive I've ever attempted.

I know now that I didn't think things out thoroughly when setting out alone to retrieve Kelly from the Jersey Devil's piney playground. If I had, I would have realized that I needed another adult along. It was bad enough that I was a distracted driver—we were lucky to make it back over the Ben Franklin Bridge in one piece—but once I got to Children's Hospital, I faced the problem of what to do with the damned car. Previously I'd always been dropped off by Alan or someone else, or Kelly had been well enough to walk with me from long-term parking and take the elevator up to the emergency room. (At least I knew that was where we were going; the CHOP system had trained me well enough so that I harbored no illusions that Kelly would be admitted as a regular patient. We were headed to Emergency, but how was I going to do this?)

Heading up Thirty-fourth Street, I turned in where I saw the Emergency sign and pulled in as far as I could, making sure to pull my tiny car well out of the way of any ambulance routes or ambulance parking. I jumped out and opened Kelly's door. By this time she was ashen, and the weakness I'd seen during the puking episode on the highway shoulder was more pronounced. She was too big for me to carry her, and when I tried to sling her arm over my shoulder and walk her along with me, she kept collapsing. I was worried she would faint, or that I would drop her. I pushed her gently back on to the back seat.

"I'll get someone," I told her, closing the door. Then I went through the automatic doors to the security desk.

"My daughter is in extreme pain. She has a failing liver. She can't walk. I need someone to come get her on a stretcher."

I had interrupted two security guys in mid-discussion. One of them turned toward me in annoyance.

"Lady, you can't park out there."

"My daughter is twelve and she's out there. It's an emergency. Can you come get her on a stretcher? She's been a patient here."

"Lady, is that your car out there? You can't park the car out there."

"Forget the car. My daughter is out there and she's too weak to walk. What are you going to do about it?"

They had no idea. It wasn't part of the security guards' job description. One of them looked down at the phone.

"I'm telling you lady, you gotta go park that car somewhere else."

"MY KID IS SICK! SOMEONE HAS TO HELP ME GET HER IN HERE!"

"There's a wheelchair over there, lady, but I don't know. You better move your car."

I walked over to a dark corner where two battered wheelchairs sat, their front wheels butting up against each other. I tried to pull one away from the other and got them more tangled. Then I realized that both chairs were in the locked position. Eventually I managed to free one as the men looked on, showing no intention of helping.

I walked the chair to the door, pushed the automatic door opener, and went out to the car. I am terrible with equipment, especially wheelchairs, and no amount of practicing with Alan during his crippled time had made me much better. After a few unsuccessful tries, I finally got the sequence right of opening Kelly's car door and then sliding the wheelchair parallel to where she was sitting in the back seat. I had to grab her around the middle to get her over and around the wheelchair arm and on to the seat, but my pulling reactivated her pain *and* the screaming. By the time I was wheeling her inside, she was throwing up again. As I pushed her to the emergency room front desk, the less vociferous guard now joined in the warnings.

"Hey, *lady*. You can't leave your car out there. They're gonna tow it."

I ignored him and started filling out the usual paperwork as Kelly retched behind me.

"My child is vomiting," I said as calmly as I could to the front desk clerk. "Does anyone have an emesis basin?"

"Not here," said the clerk, as Kelly threw up a big piece of puke near my feet. I looked down and saw a dirty syringe next to the vomit.

"Fine," I said. "Kelly, don't you worry about anything. I want you to scream your head off. Go ahead and throw up all you want." The indifference around us made me want to scream. Probably people who work around sick kids all day long become inured to the conditions.

I signed the papers and then wheeled Kelly over to the waiting area with the cutesy health video games. It wasn't even suppertime yet, and the waiting area was unusually quiet. The acoustics of the atrium were superb: You could hear the pinging and the video soundtracks, and, clear as a bell, the sound of my child vomiting and screaming.

I called friends and my mom while we waited the usual interminable time to see a doctor. I knew Kelly was really sick because she wanted nothing—no water, no food, not even any physical attention. She'd be quiet for a while, and then the screaming and vomiting would resume. I don't think I've ever felt more useless. It was more than an hour before we were called into the triage area.

That's when my battle with the security guards escalated. The taller one freaked out that I was disappearing from sight without having moved my car.

"Lady, I'm warning you. It's gonna cost you."

"I am with my very sick child. I am the only adult here. I am *not* going to leave her side to move the car."

"You could just pull it down to the garage. You gotta pull it down to the garage."

I started to feel as if I were talking on some high-frequency undetectable to human ears. "I am *not* going anywhere. My child needs me, and I am staying here. The garage is far away. Now, here's some money, if one of you wants to move it."

The guard recoiled from the two rumpled twenty-dollar bills I had pulled from my pocket. "Can't, lady. Against the rules."

"Okay. I don't give a fuck, then. Tow it. Go ahead. Call them."

It was more than an hour before a liver doctor came to see Kelly, and it was while Kelly was being examined that I finally slipped away and moved the car to the lower level of the parking garage. No one had touched it; there wasn't even a ticket or a note on the windshield. I was frantic during the almost twenty minutes it took to do it, thinking the whole time that I should have forgotten about it. But by the time I got back, someone had started a morphine drip for Kelly's pain.

Kelly stood by her initial description: She felt as if there were a bone in her vagina, stabbing her. Sometimes it hurt when she moved, and sometimes when she stayed still. I submitted to the usual questions and retold the story of Kelly's AIH. Kelly was submitted to a battery of blood tests and physical examinations.

By the time my mother appeared at the door of our exam cubicle, two female interns were attempting to talk Kelly into a pelvic exam. My twelve-year-old kid's alabaster legs were in stirrups, and she was contracting her hips back toward her body with all her might. She had started to whimper when she realized that the doctors intended to put something up her vagina.

"Relax, Kelly," said one of them.

"Relax, and it won't hurt!" said the other, moving quickly toward Kelly's crotch with a metal speculum.

My mother was appalled. "She's too young for this," she whispered. Kelly was gripping my hand and beginning to cry harder, and I felt the tears gathering in the corners of my eyes, too.

The next course of action to determine the cause of Kelly's pain was a kidney ultrasound, because they suspected a kidney stone. I'd heard about the pain caused by kidney stones but knew nothing about them. In the next few weeks, Kelly and I would find out all about the pain caused by these tiny granules of calcium and other minerals.

The ultrasound didn't show anything, but one of the nurses told me it wasn't surprising—kidney stones often don't show up in ultrasound screenings. But Kelly's pain, nausea, and fever were enough to justify admittance, so Kelly found herself once again an inpatient at Children's Hospital. This time, though, we were on the nephrology floor. The mom cots were comfier on this floor. (Why, I wondered? Were there more parents of older children?) I felt like a fish out of water. In the other two hospitalizations, I'd managed to get the lay of the land. Now I was once again in strange territory. Funny how you cling to the organs to which you're assigned: Kelly and I were used to being in the liver group. Why, now, would her kidneys suddenly go? It was the kidneys, the bloody urine, that had initially led us into the nether world of Children's Hospital, but for the past six months she'd been coping with being a liver patient. And now we had been unceremoniously introduced to another organ. The kidneys made the liver look almost glamorous.

The next day Kelly had a kidney CT scan, which is where the stone showed up. These "stones" are tiny things, minuscule pebbles made up of minerals that should have been washed away in the body's bloodstream and subsequent streams of liquid. When the body's ability to process such minerals malfunctions, little stones appear and sometimes have difficulty making their way down the various tubes from the kidney to the urethra, or outside entrance of the bladder. The tiny stones can shift around—which accounts for why they hurt—and then sometimes can pass unnoticed to the outside. Many people probably pass these tiny stones on any given day; it's just when things goes wrong and they hurt that we notice them.

I really liked the "crack" nephrologist who showed up the next day. Dr. Stockman. She was kind, attentive, and worried about Kelly's pain. She listened patiently to my stories about Thailand and how the problem with Kelly's liver had begun. I had gone home for a few hours the day before while my mother stayed with Kelly, and in that time I'd looked up as many things as I could think of, including links between any of Kelly's drugs and kidney stones. I was not that surprised when I started to see connections between massive doses of prednisone and kidney stones. But in all our time at Children's Hospital, only Dr. Stockman agreed that prednisone could have been the trigger. The other liver specialists and kidney doctors said that the evidence for such a connection was only anecdotal.

I hate it when doctors dismiss your questions by saying that a piece of evidence is only anecdotal. Of course it is. For the most part, there is not enough money to fund studies on everything, and I knew for certain that no one was wasting time and money to find out how many people who took prednisone later developed kidney stones. Yet I've heard from so many for whom that happened. Just calling around or hanging around on the Internet, I'd found dozens of people with AIH who'd reported problems with kidney stones, and people with asthma and MS who'd also been dosed with high amounts of steroids who'd reported kidney stones as a natural side effect.

The word on the street is that kidney stones are the only condition that gives childbirth a run for its money in the pain department, and this became a joke with Kelly. "Now I can have a baby because I know what it feels like," she said. Years before, I'd known a grown man with kidney stones who'd said that the pain reduced him to fits of insanity that not even Vicodin could help.

This time, Kelly spent five days in the hospital. Some days were better than others. One day I got the one kidney intern, Dr. Brown, to admit that kidney stones constantly shifted, so I could understand how Kelly was at times in excruciating pain and at other times, well, "okay."

The idea was to get Kelly to pass the stone. Waiting it out was traditionally done with adults, and it seemed a good, if painful, plan. But when it came to kids, well, not so much. Actually, there was no plan for kids, as I found out. Children seldom suffer from kidney stones. So what were we supposed to do?

The expert in the kind of kidney stone Kelly had was next door, at the Hospital of the University of Pennsylvania (HUP). But right away I was told that Kelly couldn't see the adult expert, who never took pediatric patients. This made me mad. Why couldn't I just walk next door with Kelly's records and find out what we should do about her kidney stone?

I'd always heard that CHOP had a great pain management team, but even in this, our third hospitalization, we didn't see any sign of them. During the kidney stone attack, Kelly needed constant morphine, and a pump would have been ideal. Even though I requested one, no pain management specialists ever came to examine her. Instead, the nursing staff timed out her morphine tablets to the exact minute, which meant that, in an ideal world, she would get a new dose of pain relief every four hours. But we were caught in the imperfect world—that is CHOP—so the pain-relief-dispensing system seemed like a total farce. I could always tell that the morphine was beginning to wear off in the fourth hour: Kelly would begin to thrash around and get whiney and demanding. Sometimes I'd point out to the nursing staff that they should order the morphine from the pharmacy *before* it began to wear off, but evidently that was against the rules. Instead, the nurse in charge would order the morphine at exactly the time Kelly was supposed to be taking it, and then the pharmacy would take its sweet time delivering the medication to our floor. In the best-case scenario the meds would arrive only about forty-five minutes late, but it wasn't unusual for Kelly to go up to two hours past when the morphine level in her bloodstream was beginning to drop. Then it would take another hour for the morphine level in her bloodstream to get to the point where it could relieve her pain adequately—so basically she was in a lot of pain for about half her waking time, and it seemed mostly due to the hospital's stupid and inefficient way of dispensing pain medication.

During this hospital stay, I found myself seething and complaining more than I ever had. For a child who had never even experienced menstrual cramps, the pain in Kelly's hips, lower back, and crotch was mysterious and frightening. My mother and I spent hours holding her feverish head and stroking her back and stomach. I couldn't stand not being able to get my child out of pain and knowing that if we were at home she'd be more comfortable with the same drugs administered thoughtfully and on time. I made a mental note then and there, too, that I would somehow manage to keep a store of morphine or Vicodin at home so that I could give it to Kelly at the first sign of pain from a kidney stone.

After discussing kidney stones again with the nephrology team, I brought up the dirty *s* word—*surgery.* They didn't recommend it, and neither did the kind surgeon who came by to see Kelly one day.

"Most of these things do dissolve or pass, but they hurt like heck, there's no denying it." I liked this guy—he looked me straight in the eye and had one of those generic Southern-style voices some people call an army accent. Dr. Cypres was your usual macho surgeon type with a bit of a sensitive side, exactly the kind of doctor who should work with children.

"If she can tough it out, then that would be great. With adults, of course, they can handle the pain differently, and the time doesn't seem as endless. If this gets too much for her, though, I would go in and get it."

"Get it?"

"Yes. We go up through the urethra with an instrument that has a little basket on it. We can see it on the ultrasound, and then we can get the basket around it and pull the stone out."

The surgeon shared something with us before he left Kelly's room that day. "I know it hurts," he said to Kelly, "and thanks to my wife I can really understand just how much. She gets these stones all the time, and I watch her suffer. I never really knew before I met her, what it was like. So if this gets too bad for you, you just call, and I'll take it out."

For now, though, we'd go home the next day and see if Kelly could drink lots of water and pass the stone naturally. The water thing was crucial, the nurses kept saying, and of course this was beginning to be a problem, because although Kelly naturally drank a lot of liquids, once she figured out that she was *supposed to* drink gallons of water, she stopped touching the stuff. It wasn't a problem here in the hospital, because she was on a constant intravenous drip of saline solution. But out in the real world of our home, that meant I was going to have to harass her constantly.

That night at about ten o'clock, the room phone rang (weird, because all incoming calls were turned off at nine) and I picked it up. It was the security guard from downstairs.

"There is a Mr. James Schank here at the desk. He says he's come in from out of town and insists that he be allowed to come up. Shall I send him up?"

"Jimmy!" Kelly shrieked as our good and fairly demented friend from Washington poked his neatly coifed head in the door. He had just driven up and was not about to miss Kelly just because of something as silly as visiting hours. He'd brought a bag of junk food and candy and a teen-girl magazine with hundreds of pictures of actors starring in bad WB and Fox television shows. For some reason we couldn't figure out, a "hunky" picture of Regis Philbin was on one spread right in the midst of all the teenagers and twentysomethings.

"Regis is for your grandmother," said Jimmy. He and Kelly looked so cute evaluating the chests and buns of the guys. An hour before, Kelly's face had sagged with weariness. Now she was laughing so loud I thought the nurses would come kick Jimmy out.

But Jimmy was a wonderful tonic for Kelly—by being silly, by scarfing down Cheetos and rating boys, he'd made her forget the needles and tubes.

6. Hospital Days

A hospital is no place to be sick.

Samuel Goldwyn

The hospital days seemed endless and interchangeable, and yet they had a certain rhythm that the days at home lacked. Kelly and I clung to the rituals we established whenever we were at CHOP. I brought nice quilts and pillows and dozens of videos, and snack foods, soda, and bottled water. Kelly's father brought picnic dinners from our local gourmet shop and my mother brought in pizzas and cut-up vegetables. One night Mom even sneaked in some chardonnay in a plastic juice bottle and she and I drank it out of paper cups with our McDonald's hamburgers. After a long day of putting up with the parade of uncooperative doctors, it felt heavenly, like liquid peace.

The small television mounted on the wall was our hearth, the focus of our day's rhythms. Kelly had been too young when the hospital show *ER* was first on, but now it was on for a solid two hours each morning, and we gobbled up the episodes. The irony of it didn't escape us, of course—why would we care about the problems of a fictional hospital when we were stuck inside a real one?

"Mom, there's not a single doctor here who is even half as nice as the ones on *ER*," Kelly said one day during a commercial, unlocking for me the mystery of the show's allure. I had sworn that after accompanying Alan on an emergency helicopter ride, where I watched the doctors "bag him," a term they were always using on *ER*, I would never watch another medical show again. But however realistic the TV hospital was supposed to be, it was still a fantasy I kept getting pulled back into. Spending two hours with the doctors and patients on *ER* was a picnic compared to being in a real hospital.

Once *ER* was over, we'd switch to Animal Planet, our favorite. We didn't get the channel on our cable system at home, and so were completely susceptible to its charms: twenty-four hours of programming about emergency veterinarian hospitals, dog breeds, dogs with jobs, vanishing species, and animals that did funny tricks or played musical instruments. Kelly and I hadn't known Animal Planet existed until our first time at CHOP. It reminded us immediately of our trip to London, where every day we would return to our hotel to recover from sightseeing and get ready to go out to the theater. Dozing on our little single beds in our bare room, we'd watch two animal-emergency shows back to back. There was a sheep recovering from smoke inhalation, and a squirrel that needed mouth-to-mouth resuscitation. The narrator's voice was low-key but intense, and made you really care about whether Fluffy was going to make it. Those were the stories we loved most on Animal Planet, too—the emergencies. I started developing routines about them.

"Oh, yeah, here we are in the hospital because Kelly has a life-threatening disease, but all we care about is the chipmunk who needs CPR," I'd say. Kelly got sick of hearing it and began to step all over my routines.

"Not that joke again, Mom," she said.

I found I couldn't sleep in the mom cot unless I kept the television on all night, but I usually dozed for only two or three hours. I read a lot, using one of those itty-bitty book lights I'd brought from home. Kelly slept a lot, at all times of the day and night. The doctors came on rounds at around six A.M. and always woke us. At first I was embarrassed, as if I were supposed to wake up quickly and cheerfully when a young intern touched my shoulders. After a while I almost always managed to stir right before they entered the room, as if I could sense the herd coming to ask us even more questions. I hated trying to get information from them when I was so vulnerable. I don't know about you, but the absolute first thing I have to do when I wake up is urinate. So there I'd be, addled, tousled, sweaty (since I was already starting to have pre-menopausal night sweats), and desperately having to pee, trying to hold my own with four or five doctors in crisp white coats staring me down. I would have been a lot more assertive in any other situation, which explains why I allowed the long-haired female nephrologist intern to metaphorically piss all over me one morning.

I had met this intern, Dr. Brown, a few times during Kelly's other hospitalizations. She was one of the scary interns who had attempted a pelvic examination on Kelly in the emergency room. I had never seen her crack a smile, not even one of those fake ones used by most doctors at Children's Hospital to lure kids into thinking they were nice.

This time, Kelly was again displaying signs of a bladder infection, and of course the blood in her urine still pointed to some sort of kidney trouble, even though everyone was stymied about what it could possibly be.

I had one agenda during this meeting: I wanted to get someone to say that it was okay for Kelly to take Pyridium, a drug that soothes the urinary tract. Many women who suffer from frequent urinary tract infections take it. Pyridium doesn't cure, but it helps relieve that awful irritated feeling. You can buy it over the counter, and I'd considered just giving it to Kelly even though I knew it wasn't recommended for anyone with liver problems. But Kelly's liver problems were in abeyance, and I'd already gotten a gastroenterologist the day before to say she couldn't see the harm in Pyridium. The only problem was that she hadn't written it on Kelly's chart. I'd used Pyridium myself, so I knew that the real reason I couldn't just slip one of the tiny pills to Kelly was that it turns urine bright orange.

Dr. Brown listened to my request, formed haltingly as I tried to wake up, and denied it, of course, because no one in gastroenterology had signed off on it.

"Your daughter has to keep hydrated," Dr. Brown said. "How much water is she drinking a day? You have to push the liquids."

"She's having trouble with that. She's twelve, you know. The whole pre-adolescent thing. It's almost as if, since she found out she has to drink more water, she won't do it."

Dr. Brown started sputtering. "You have to *make* her drink the water. This is serious. It's not optional. If you don't do it, you're a negligent parent. It's as if you let her smoke, or let her get behind the wheel of a car."

I was stunned into silence. I couldn't believe she'd used the words *negligent parent*. I felt as if my brain were full of jelly, but somewhere in the jelly there was a statement forming that would never make it to my vocal cords: "Oh yeah? Well, you're a negligent *person*!"

The team left and I dashed into the bathroom to relieve myself, but of course I couldn't do it immediately because the "bonnet" collecting Kelly's bloody urine was still on the toilet. The nurses had not shown up for the twenty-four-hour collection. On the floor was another bonnet filled with feces. I felt like screaming. The hospital was hot and humid, and the bathroom reeked. It was all I could do to keep from kicking the fecal bonnet around the floor.

I came out of the filthy bathroom and climbed back into the tiny, uncomfortable mom cot. It was low to the ground so that I could gaze up at Kelly, fast asleep once again. Exhausted, I thought I could drift back to sleep, but the image of Dr. Brown saying I was endangering my kid kept roiling around my brain. Before I knew it, I was on my feet and out at the nurses' station.

"What is the name of the supervisor of that doctor who was just here?" I said to the nurse behind the desk.

"Which doctor?"

"The nephrologist. Dr. Brown. I want to know the name of her supervisor. She insulted me. She was insulting and rude, and I will talk to her supervisor. I'm a writer, a journalist, and I will contact the head of this hospital about this. I need this information immediately."

"Okay," the nurse said. I thought I saw her shaking her head slightly.

Kelly has mythologized the next scene in our family life. Once, when she and I attended a conference in Tampa about brain injury, the physical and occupational therapists we met from the sponsoring institution, the Veteran's Hospital, persuaded her to talk at the panel on traumatic brain injury and family life.

"I was too young to remember how my mom handled my dad's brain injury," said the fourteen-year-old Kelly, "but when *I* was in the hospital, she kicked ass!"

Gales of laughter came up from the audience.

"No, really," Kelly said. "We have a saying in our family that there's always one person who has to be there at the hospital when someone's sick. We call her 'the lady with the purse.' " (This is actually our friend Joellen's phrase.)

"And that was my mom, the lady with the purse, who sits on the end of the bed and asks obnoxious questions. And one time my mom even made a doctor apologize, and that really *rocked*."

Yes. I really did get Dr. Brown to apologize. About an hour after I pulled my scene out at the nurse's station, someone came in to roust me from my cot once again, although, truth be told, I'd never gotten close to falling back to sleep.

"Mrs. Crimmins? It's Dr. Brown. I heard you wanted to speak to my supervisor?"

Did I ever. Dr. Brown agreed to meet with me herself in the next few minutes. When she came back, I erupted.

"I'm very upset by the way you addressed me before. You have to understand what it's like to have a preteen daughter, chronically ill, and everything we've been through—"

"Mrs. Crimmins," the doctor interrupted. "Please. Let's find a place to go discuss this." Kelly looked up at me from an episode of *ER*, which had just begun.

"I'll be right back," I said to her.

Dr. Brown and I went around the corner and found a small conference room off the hallway. I sat on one side of the table, and she on the other.

"Look," I said.

"No, no, please, let me say something," the doctor said. Her cockiness was gone, and suddenly she looked like a high-school girl in detention.

"I'm sorry. I don't know why I talked to you that way," she said. "I had no right."

I have a bad character flaw that surfaces when people try to apologize: I talk all over them.

"I resent being called a negligent parent," I said, cutting her off.

"No, no, please," the doctor said. "Please let me say that I don't know why I did that. Maybe I'm tired. As soon as I left you I felt badly about it. Let me tell you, I apologize."

I can't say it ever turned warm and sunny with us. She tried to relate to me, even confessing that she'd had urinary tract infections and knew how uncomfortable they were. She would call Kelly's gastroenterologists that day and get permission to give her the Pyridium. She didn't see where it would be a problem.

Then we discussed encouraging Kelly to drink lemonade. I told her how hard this whole experience had been, and how I thought Kelly was feeling a bit battered, and I was, too. I started crying when I mentioned that Kelly had already gone through the tragedy of her father's accident, and now was facing her own disease. Had the doctor not noticed the side effects of the prednisone, how my kid was now almost one hundred pounds over her normal weight?

"Yes," she said. "I'm sorry. I want to help your daughter."

When I got back to the room, Kelly wanted all the details, but I found the story anticlimactic, and my narrative abilities seemed shut off. The doctor had folded, basically. I'd become a giant inflated anger monster, and she'd deflated my anger quickly and efficiently. And yet the whole episode hadn't led to any real bonding—it's not as if I felt the doctor had taken a new interest in us or our problems. More likely, I felt she was just trying to save her ass.

But in the years since, Kelly refers to the incident often, so it must have impressed her. "My mom made a doctor apologize," she says. "Not many people can make one do that."

After her first two hospitalizations, Kelly's case had switched organs—her liver numbers had become normal, but her kidneys were a mess. She was still peeing blood, which no one could figure out, and she needed a twenty-four-hour collection of urine *and* a kidney biopsy. She had moved from the land of gastroenterology to the land of nephrology.

I knew enough about biopsies from the liver episode that I didn't buy the soft sell. The biopsy was going to hurt, and it was going to bother Kelly. It wasn't as easy as all the doctors and nurses said. Specifically, I didn't want Kelly to have to suffer with that drug, Versed, which had not put her out and had given her a physical allergic reaction. I found out the name of the surgeon performing the procedure and called his office three times. Of course I never was able to talk to him, but I left a message each time saying I didn't want my daughter to have Versed during the procedure.

The kidney biopsy was the pinnacle of our unpleasant experiences at CHOP. That time they at least got my request for pain relief right, which made all the difference afterward. The pain management team came to see us the night before and made arrangements for Kelly to have a morphine pump that would continuously supply morphine. The pump was set to dispense a constant amount, and on top of that, Kelly could choose to push it whenever she felt she needed more.

But there were stumbling blocks before we got to the actual operation. For one, an anesthesiologist came around in pre-op to tell us what would happen, and when he said that Kelly would be sedated with a mild sedative not unlike Valium, I said that I knew it wouldn't be Versed, since I had specifically asked several times that they find something else.

"No, we're using Versed, according to the chart," he said.

"That's not possible. My daughter is allergic to Versed, and I've asked that it not be used."

"No, it says Versed here. What's the big deal? We always use Versed in adolescent girls."

"My daughter had a violent reaction to that drug. You can't use it. She's allergic to it."

"I've never heard of anyone who is allergic to Versed," the doctor said. "It's not true."

"But my daughter *is* allergic. She had a very violent reaction to the drug."

"That's not possible."

"Several nurses at this hospital, and one doctor, told me that it was possible," I said. "You are not using Versed."

"Yes, we are," the doctor said.

I took a step toward him and did something I'd never done before or since. I screamed incomprehensible syllables in his face, at the top of my lungs. The hustle and bustle of the room stopped immediately.

"I can see you are frustrated," he said, smirking. "What is it you want?"

"I want you to say you're not using Versed during the operation."

"Okay. We won't use Versed. Are you happy?"

"Very."

One fuckup per operation should be the rule, but, alas, that wasn't going to be the case here. Kelly had already had a preoperative injection with a tranquilizer, and a nice young social worker had come over to talk to me. Then, out of nowhere, a Chinese anesthesiologist approached me while I was chatting with the social worker. He didn't seem to speak much English.

"I give your son injection," he said.

Now, I know this might seem weird, but I'd gotten used to medical personnel from other countries getting their pronouns confused, so I didn't think much of of the fact that he had called Kelly my son.

"An injection? Are you sure? No, my daughter has already been treated."

"No, I give injection," he said, smiling.

"*No!*" It was the young social worker who pushed the Chinese anesthesiologist away and took the chart out of his hands.

"Look at this chart," she said. "Here, look. You are supposed to be with a *male* patient, a seventeen-year-old African American boy. Kelly is white, twelve years old. Does she look like your patient?"

I felt my knees buckle a bit. Sure, the injection probably wouldn't have killed her, but this was a new low in Children's Hospital care. The Chinese physician giggled inappropriately and slid off.

"Thank you," I said to the social worker. Her face turned red, and she, too, moved away. It wasn't a moment of triumph for her; more like one of horror. At least I didn't have to work in this environment, I thought. No, I was the Mother, and all I had to do was stand around and scream and hope that the medical personnel around me would be able to tell the difference between a twelve-year-old white female and a seventeen-year-old African American boy.

I had asked to be with Kelly during the kidney biopsy, since the liver biopsy had been so disturbing. This time I saw exactly what happened during such a procedure. Kelly never really succumbed to the sedation. It was peculiar, certainly, but undeniably one of her biological quirks. Surely there must be some people for whom regular sedation just doesn't work, and my kid was one of them.

"Now you'll feel a little pinch," said the doctor.

"Ouch!" Kelly said. "Ow, ouch, ow ow ow."

"Now, you can't feel that, Kelly," he said.

"Yes, I can! What are you doing now?"

"Nothing, Miss Kelly. Nothing. We're taking some pictures now."

"Ow! You're cutting me! I can feel it! It's like there are scissors there."

I watched and saw the doctor put the long scissors into the incision. Yes, he was snipping a piece of her kidney off. Pictures, my ass!

The doctor was getting nervous because Kelly was becoming more vocal. At least the procedure was short, and soon Kelly was being wheeled out of the operating room and into recovery. Just as with the liver biopsy recovery, she was crying.

"She should be asleep," a nurse said.

"Well, she's not," I said. "She doesn't seem to go to sleep during these kinds of things, even though no one believes us."

I'd have to nominate the kidney biopsy as worse than the liver, because for days afterward, Kelly had nerve pain in her left leg.

Shooting pain, she said. I paged the doctor once right afterward and again the next day.

"No," he said both times he examined her. "The type of nerve pain she's describing can't possibly be related to the biopsy."

"It happens all the time with the kidney biopsy," one nurse told me. "They nick a nerve as they're going in, and you get some pain in the leg for a while afterward."

Are hospitals designed to make you crazy? How can one person deny and another affirm, and yet you can't hold either one responsible for their comments? I began to think I should be wired, to record everything these people said to me. I didn't want money or retribution; I just wanted to know I wasn't going crazy accompanying my daughter to what was supposed to be a simple procedure and then finding out that there were sometimes side effects. It's always easier to deal with something if you are informed, so why did this particular system feel it was best to keep everyone in the dark?

Kelly's nerve pain went away after a few days, and this time the morphine pump made things a bit easier. Kelly and I argued about how often she should push it, though, with me encouraging her to push it often. Sometimes I'd see her presumably asleep and I'd push it once, making it beep.

"Mom!" Kelly would say, half asleep. "Stop it!"

"Oh, shut up, little Judy," I would say, making her giggle. Long ago we'd started making jokes about the young Judy Garland. Sick, I know. But what can I say? Those of us dwelling perpetually in the sick zone eventually *become* sick, and we can't help ourselves.

Kelly left the hospital a day after the kidney biopsy. It was the dog days of August, and we settled in back home, hoping that her kidney stone would pass on its own. She was unhappy not to be able to go back to camp—but, really, how could she? At any moment the stone could shift again and she would be in horrifying, nauseating pain.

Five months earlier, when she was diagnosed, I'd called our cable company and ordered the full package. So what if I didn't have the money? Screw it. Now we would have everything: HBO, Showtime, Cinemax, Starz, etc. The only thing that kept Kelly from thinking about pain was watching movies. I'd already flunked Video Rental 101 by always having to pay enormous late fees. Kelly's thing was to watch the same movie over and over again, like most of her friends, and so signing up for every premium channel known to man seemed the natural thing to do.

And so, let the cable TV begin! I kept trying to liquidate Kelly, plying her with homemade lemonade, sparkling water, diet and regular sodas, and she stayed in bed watching hours and hours of movies. Once in a while I would sit with her and we'd talk about the stupid little calcium crystal that was stuck inside her. It was so frustrating to know that she couldn't shake or press it out. We had to wait and hope it would dislodge itself and float down the tube into her urethra and then out into the toilet.

Unfortunately, on the fourth day the pain "popped," forcing its way through the morphine and into the forefront of her consciousness and my concerns. Kelly tried to be brave, but the nausea returned. It was time, I decided. How much longer could we make her suffer? An adult might be able to withstand the pain and the wait to get rid of the kidney stone, but why should we make a twelve-year-old suffer this much? I waited one more day and then called the kindly kidney surgeon who had said he understood.

We were back in the hospital two days later, with the surgery scheduled for the following day. I was impressed that the doctor had been willing to operate on a Saturday. The surgery went well, but I hadn't realized that they would put a stent in the tube where they'd extracted the stone. And Kelly had to be catheterized for a few days afterward.

To put it simply, Kelly felt violated. The tubes sticking out of her vagina freaked her out, as did the bloody mess dripping into her catheter bag. Yet the stone was gone and, eventually, the pain would be, too.

We left the hospital two days later, and only another two days after that we were off to Rochester, Minnesota, for our first experience at the world-famous Mayo Clinic.

7. The Road to Mayo

"Faith" is a fine invention
When gentlemen can see;
But Microscopes are prudent
In an Emergency.

Emily Dickinson

"The Mayo Clinic is like the secular equivalent of going to Lourdes," says Joellen, one of Kelly's three unofficial godmothers. I think she's right. The Mayo Clinic has passed into American mythology as the last resort of hopeless cases. It has the exotic reputation as healer to the famous and foreign. It was the place the Shah of Iran went when he was ailing, one of the pop culture references my brain dredged up when Kelly and I sat in the Mayo waiting room watching a sheikh and his entourage who were gathered in the corner.

When I began to tell people that I was taking Kelly to the Mayo Clinic, their first reaction was disbelief. First, said some, they didn't know you could actually just *go* there. Didn't you have to be referred to the Mayo Clinic by other doctors? Others, also registering disbelief, had shown enormous concern. It was if they hadn't believed before that Kelly was *that* sick. Gosh, if you're going to Mayo, she must be dying or something. I even began scaring myself by talking about it. Was it really necessary? Was I being melodramatic?

My mom had been a tremendous help, handling all the travel arrangements. She had decided to come along, to help in any way she could, and I really appreciated it. After the experience of driving Kelly to an emergency room solo, I never wanted to be caught in a situation where I'd have to leave Kelly alone in a hospital setting.

We had told Kelly's doctors that we'd be taking her on a plane in a few days, and they'd okayed the trip, especially considering the destination. I'm sure it would have been different if we'd been proposing a vacation. But this was a medical visit, and once we got to Minnesota, we would be fairly safe. What could be safer than hanging out at a world-famous clinic?

Just to make the trip a bit more surreal, though, we made a pit stop at the Mall of America, the world's largest mall, which is just outside Minneapolis and off the interstate highway that leads to Rochester, where the Mayo Clinic is located. The mall isn't far from the airport, either, so even though we're not "mall" people, I thought it would be fun to take Kelly there for some shopping before we hit the clinic. For our first night in Minnesota, I found a motel right across the street from the mall. Kelly had been sick so often, she'd not really been shopping for a while.

Okay, as I've said, I'm not a mall person. Actually, I *hate* malls. In my worst fears, hell looks just like the Mall of America in Minnesota.

As for my decision to go there, I plead temporary insanity. My crazed shopping plan shows how much a person's attitude can change when she thinks her kid might die. With Kelly's illness, I began to embrace the maudlin. In between hospitalizations, I'd even given in to Kelly's fascination with the Build-A-Bear shop in the Plymouth Meeting Mall near Philadelphia, taking her and her friend Maddy there and dropping about a hundred and fifty bucks so that they could construct two teddy bears and outfit them in frilly dresses. I started crying when Maddy put a message into the stuffing in Kelly's toy saying she wished most of all for Kelly to be well.

Yes, Kelly's illness was making me go as soft in the head as that bear's stuffing. It hadn't been necessary to tell her about the Mall of America at all, but I was starting to function like a one-woman Make-A-Wish Foundation. I was going to give my sick kid as good a time as I possibly could, and since I knew that once we got to Mayo there would be scores of blood tests, ultrasounds, X-rays and other indignities, I wanted her to just be a kid for a day.

In retrospect, I was trying too hard, and almost everything I did malfunctioned. Only minutes after we'd parked our rental car, Mom and Kelly and I left our corny Country Suites motel and picked our way across the various entry ramps to get to the mall. Only urbanites like us would think it was possible to walk to a monstrosity such as the Mall of America from anywhere, even from across the street, because even though the mall *looked* as if it were across the street, it was really pedestrian miles away. It was almost a hundred degrees that first afternoon we arrived, and so by the time we'd dodged traffic and shuttle buses and found the proper entrance, all three of us were like limp dishrags.

I might not like malls, but I do love hokey stuff. In my time I've been a connoisseur of Americana kitsch, so I was up for this place with its giant Kellogg's cornflakes exhibits, John Deere toy tractor shops, and especially its Minnesota-themed emporiums featuring stuffed moose toys and cheese hats. I had seen polyurethane cheese hats in Wisconsin before, and now here was the Minnesota version. I tried to make Kelly try some on, but she only wanted to go into clothing shops, and that was where the trouble, and all the tears, began.

Kelly had not been allowing herself to absorb the reality of how much weight she'd gained over the past five months, or to think much about how she looked with her new prednisone "moon" face, huge arms, and the hair-tufted hunchback. I hadn't, either. I had practiced, for months, keeping my face in a neutral position whenever I saw Kelly enter a room. When I wasn't around her, I imagined her as she'd looked only last February, before all the madness began. It had been especially difficult ever since I started losing faith in the "bully" drug, to make sure she took *all* the prednisone. Even more than two months after the opportunistic herpes infection, she still had a nasty scar on her shoulder, and from looking around on the Internet and talking to others who'd experienced prednisone side effects, I felt convinced that the kidney stones had been caused by the bully drug, too.

Nothing fit Kelly in any shop. Here she was, in a place filled with cute back-to-school clothes, and not a single item was the right size for her now distorted body. Watching her weep as she couldn't even pull an extra-large T-shirt over her bloated upper arms, I wished more than ever that the last few months hadn't happened, that I'd stood my ground and not been intimidated when Dr. Palmer insisted that the prednisone dose stay at sixty milligrams. She'd said that dropping the dose could have caused Kelly to flare up and even die. Maybe she was right, but I wasn't convinced. In all the reading I'd been doing, I'd never heard of anyone who'd been on more than twenty milligrams for more than three or four months. Dr. Palmer had said that she wanted

Kelly to stay on the sixty-milligram dose for eighteen months, and if there was only one thing I wanted our visit to the Mayo Clinic to accomplish, it was that we could begin to wean her off prednisone. Her liver numbers had been close to normal after only four months on the gargantuan dose.

Kelly's crying continued, off and on, for all five days of our Mayo Clinic visit. I'd never seen her so blue before. After our unsuccessful shopping trip, we halfheartedly went out to a steakhouse-type place in yet another corporate mall and then crept into bed at our Country Suites nest. The next day we set out on the very flat and straight two-hour trip to Rochester.

The Mall of America had already opened Kelly's eyes to all her physical changes, and when we got to Rochester, it was if she'd been clobbered by the second half of a one-two punch: Everything about Rochester, Minnesota, convinced Kelly, finally, that she was really sick.

"Everyone is so old here," she said, and she was right. People might call the state of Florida God's Waiting Room, but it is an even more accurate description of the Mayo Clinic in Rochester, Minnesota. As places for sick people go, it's a brilliant setup: an underground village with all pathways leading to the various hospitals and clinics, which are all connected. Everything is built on a huge scale, and no wait is very long. The waiting rooms look like giant airline terminals, with countless rows of comfortable chairs or couches stretching by the dozens over well-carpeted surfaces. There are wheelchairs all over the Mayo Clinic and all over Rochester itself, including in all private hotels and restaurants. It's a wheelchair honor system: Patients and their caregivers can simply pick one up or drop one off anytime.

Everyone in Rochester is incredibly nice in that stereotypical Midwestern way, and it takes a while to realize that it isn't fake. Once we arrived at our first "desk," Kelly was entered into the Mayo system with a special number. I don't know whether it was chilling or comforting, but she'd have that Mayo ID number for life. The hospital magazines in the waiting rooms were filled with stories of Mayo "lifers" who returned again and again for treatment of their rare illnesses. The Mayo system is a high-tech version of how the medical world used to function. The patient, after consulting with clinic operators, decides what is her principal health issue and then is routed through that department. In Kelly's case, her initial contact would be with pediatric gastroenterology. But thanks to contacts I'd made through speaking at medical conventions, she was also going to have access to the adult specialists in her disease, and because of her problems with kidney stones, she would also see a pediatric nephrologist.

Back in the early days of August, before Kelly was forced to leave her primitive camp, I'd traveled to Atlanta, Georgia, to speak at the national brain injury conference. It was the darkest of days, and I was having a lot of trouble hiding my emotions from others. I didn't sleep at all the night before my speech, and I remember having one of those horrible menopausal sweats in the course of the presentation. I was comforted in the lady's restroom by a fellow "menopausoid," who loaned me her battery-powered mini-fan.

I guess I did an okay job of getting my message about brain injury across, but I'd felt unusually weepy when describing Alan's accident, and I just hadn't been as sharp or as funny as I usually was as a keynote speaker. I'd done a bunch of other speeches without saying anything about Kelly's health crisis to my sponsors, but when the national director, Alan Bergman, ran into me a few hours after my speech and asked how I was, I started crying. He immediately took me into a small conference room, where I spilled the beans about the terrible stress of Kelly's illness. I was nearly bleating as I described AIH and its dangers, and then I told him that the only good news was that we would be taking Kelly to the Mayo Clinic at the end of the month.

"We have someone to help us," said Alan. "Don't you worry. I'm going to introduce you to Jim Malec at Mayo. He's part of our traumatic brain injury family, and he's going to take care of you."

Alan was true to his word. I met Jim the next day in the hotel lobby.

"I want you to write out everything you know about your daughter's illness, and then what you want to happen when you and Kelly come to Mayo, and I'm going to take care of it," Jim said. I was overwhelmed by his kindness and agreed to tour his brain injury facility while I was out at the clinic.

The one thing I wanted was to have Albert Czaja examine Kelly. He is the man who first identified the consistent symptoms that lead to AIH, basically the "father" of the disease. (Although who would want to be known as the father of any disease?) It wasn't until well after we left Mayo that I truly appreciated just what Jim Malec did for us: He used his connections to get Albert Czaja, a world-famous gastroenterologist, to see Kelly, even though she was only twelve years old.

"You know, Kelly, I don't usually see children," Dr. Czaja said during our appointment on our second day at Mayo, "but you nearly made me forget you were a child."

The doctor might have been ordered from Central Casting for a 1940s medical melodrama, in the mode of Dr. Kildare.

All of the examination rooms at the Mayo are spacious and look like settings for a Norman Rockwell painting. There is pretty wooden wainscoting along the walls, and wooden desks and old-fashioned wooden pedestals for the examination tables. Even in the ultrasound suites, there are wooden changing booths, with textured cloth curtains and little alcoves where you can put your clothes after changing into a gown.

The attitude toward appointments is also pleasantly old-fashioned, which was a shocking contrast to the high-tech environment in which you're received. When we arrived at the offices of Dr. Czaja, for example, we were given a little electronic triangle with several shapes corresponding to different doors. When a particular shape glowed, we were supposed to "walk toward the light." The sci-fi look of the devices freaked me out a bit, yet we didn't wait more than five minutes, so it was terrific. But I didn't expect to find a warm, wooden examination room beyond the glowing lights, and I certainly didn't anticipate meeting doctors who were willing to spend more than an hour per patient. Every appointment was like a retro fantasy that way—doctors who took a lot of time asking Kelly about herself, and, in two cases, even calling other doctors to ask their opinions.

Dr. Czaja, an elegant, graying, rumpled presence, spent a lot of time asking Kelly about her schoolwork. He reviewed her blood work and her sonograms and CT-scans and then began saying only positive things. We were lucky, he told us, that Kelly had type 1 AIH, and that she'd responded so well to the drug treatments. But now, he told Kelly, looking her right in the eye, "it's the drugs that are killing you, not the disease." He considered her in full remission, and it was time to wean her from both the prednisone and the Imuran, the other anti-immune drug. Kelly and I both mentioned the enormous weight gain, and he was sympathetic. "You see, now, that's another issue. At this point the weight will be making your liver fattier, too, so it's best to just feel that the AIH is behind you.

"You've had a bad time," he continued, "and what I want you to do right now is to take this thing that's happened to you, and move it from the front of your brain to the back of it." At this point he gently touched Kelly's forehead and then the back of her head. "Yes, just put it away, and live, and try not to think about it anymore."

Oh, how I wished I could call my mom in from the waiting area (she'd been too shy to come back with us). I wanted her to hear this firsthand from the man who had discovered Kelly's disease. The guy was great! At that point, I could have levitated and flown back to Philadelphia without a plane. The rest of the Mayo Clinic experience was yet to come, and we saw a bunch of other doctors, but making the pilgrimage had been worth it for Czaja alone, because he had given us permission to get Kelly off the drugs. He sent us to his colleague to develop the new drug regimen.

The next day we saw Czaja's colleague, Deborah Freese, a pediatric liver doctor. She was bemused when I told her that after our conversation with Czaja, I thought we could wean Kelly from the prednisone. Dr. Freese was the voice of reason, prescribing prednisone in two- and five-milligram tablets so that I could begin weaning Kelly very gradually from the bully drug.

Freese was particularly sympathetic, too, about the side effects prednisone had already caused.

"You feel sick to your stomach, right?" she asked Kelly at one point.

"Yeah, really sick sometimes," Kelly admitted.

"I'm going to prescribe Prilosec," said Freese. "I can't believe no one has up to this point."

Simple things that make for happier patients—that seems to be the Mayo credo. Of course Kelly had been having constant stomachaches and acid reflux, but no one at CHOP had ever thought to ask. Come to think of it, we *had* told them, but I suppose they hadn't responded. Long after we left Mayo that first time, I read one of their documents about patient-centered medical practice, and it all made sense. If we ever create the national health system we desperately need, I hope the Mayo model might be one our legislators would consider.

"It was weird. I peed and put it on the windowsill, and then a hand came out and took it away," said Kelly.

We went to several locations in the clinic to have tests performed, and each time I was more impressed. They definitely had it down to a science. Because they wanted to explore every possibility of Kelly's autoimmune disease, the pediatric gastroenterologists even called for a stool test, and my poor mom was pressed into service to cut Kelly's fecal sample, which, because she'd been on weeks of pain killers, was hard as stone. We had a weird, uneasy laugh back at our motel room as my mom attempted to slice the stool with a plastic knife from a takeout meal. "Eww, Grandma!" Kelly yelled as her rock-hard stool whizzed past her head and hit the wall.

And then there was the urine. The nephrology department had recommended a twenty-four-hour urine sample, which meant that Kelly had to travel everywhere with a huge jug. When the nurse/receptionist handed her the receptacle, Kelly was in despair.

"Yuck. I can't do this, Mom. It's going to be so embarrassing, carrying that everyplace!"

"Oh, honey," said the nurse behind the desk. "This is Rochester. Everyone carries one of those around."

She was right. Along with not even blinking an eye at wheelchairs and oxygen tanks, Rochester denizens were also accustomed to urine jugs. That night we went out to dinner and then to the movies to see *The Princess Diaries,* and I saw at least five other people lugging around pee bottles.

When a person first calls the Mayo Clinic, the operators tell you to expect you'll spend at least a week in Rochester. After the first day, Kelly and I were given a printout detailing her appointments, which included various tests scattered throughout the hospital campus, plus the initial appointments with Dr. Czaja and Dr. Freese in gastroenterology, and then others with a pediatric kidney specialist. As time went on, we would receive follow-up appointments with all the specialists before we left Mayo.

In the meantime, we tried to amuse ourselves around Rochester, and unfortunately for my mother that included her own trip to the emergency room. My mom, when she's nervous, gets very flustered, and because she doesn't have much patience with objects, she has a history of hurting herself. On our third morning in Rochester, she stabbed herself in the eye with a mascara wand, something she'd done on a few other occasions. It happened early in the morning, and she didn't want to wake me or Kelly. Instead, she walked over to the emergency room of the Mayo hospital. She had scratched her eye badly enough to need a bandage across it and constant antibiotic eyedrops. Mom was mortified. The last thing she'd wanted to do was create a problem when Kelly was the patient. Also her injury left her less in control of when we were arriving for our appointments. I'm a procrastinator who tends to run out to an appointment at the last minute; my mother is a planner who likes to be anywhere at least a half hour ahead of time. So we were bickering constantly about how long it would take us to get to the various testing departments and doctor's offices. It was rotten of me not to give in and go along with my mom's style, and I knew she was wound up about it. On the second day, after waiting what probably seemed like an endless amount of time for Kelly and me to get ready for an appointment that was only fifteen minutes away, Mom erupted, throwing a bunch of Kelly's medical papers onto the floor.

"See! I can have a tantrum, too," she yelled. "I bet you didn't think I could do something like that." She was right. I was shocked. I was supposed to be the emotional one, and she was supposed to just sit around and take it. She was supposed to be the mom, and, even though I was in my late forties, I was still the little kid who had tantrums.

And now poor Mom was part-blind, which was mostly my fault, as far as I could see, since my laissez-faire attitude toward authority was fraying her nerves. I felt guilty every time I looked at her in her eye patch.

The town of Rochester wasn't agreeing with my health, either, as it was surrounded by cornfields and filled with flowering bushes, trees, and ragweed. I've never had a worse case of hay fever in my life. My eyes and nose had turned red and filled with horrible discharges, and my throat had closed up to the point where I'd wake up in the middle of the night on my saggy motel bed gasping for breath. (One night my weary mom got up and brewed me tea to try to clear my ungrateful sinuses.) Plus, Rochester was a place that defied allergy pills. But I began to wonder if I could really be this allergic to the city. Surely this was a psychological reaction to the place? My mom stabbed herself with a mascara wand, my kid cried constantly because of her weight, and my body decided at the most inconvenient time to produce more mucus than I'd ever seen in my life. Coincidence? Probably not.

Since visiting Mayo was more like visiting a famous resort than a hospital, all of the buildings were dotted with gift shops filled with souvenirs. On one of the racks I'd seen a postcard of a Rochester water tower painted like a ripe corncob, so one afternoon, armed with the card, we went on a pilgrimage to find the tower. It was located out on one of the straight flat highways that run from the Rochester hub, past three strip malls and closer to town than I'd thought it would be. It looked much better on the postcard, and Kelly didn't even want to get out of the car to look at it. I silently prayed to the giant corncob, asking for relief from all our woes—my allergies, my mother's temporary blindness, and, above all, Kelly's autoimmune hepatitis.

"So you saw the corncob?" Dr. Kidney said to Kelly as he pressed his hands into her back, checking for swelling. He was a pediatric nephrologist with a great sense of humor, my favorite out of all the doctors we met. (Well, he had almost a hyperactive sense of humor; he was an unrelenting punster.)

"Yeah, and—"

"It looks better on the postcard, right?" he said.

Kelly laughed. Dr. Kidney was perhaps the best living example of the patient-centered approach at Mayo. He listened to everything we said and took time to process it. He was the first kidney specialist to say that the blood in Kelly's urine might not mean anything, explaining to us that some people just have that problem during various times of their lives, and they'll never know why. When I told him about the horror of the liver and kidney biopsies and the controversy over the sedative Versed, which had given Kelly that violent allergic reaction, he stroked his chin in an appropriately retro doctor way and actually seemed to believe me that Kelly was allergic to the drug.

"Wait just a second," he said, and took out what looked like a small BlackBerry-type gadget and typed into it furiously. He slumped down into his chair, leaning backward.

"Huh. Whadaya know? It says here that allergy is rare, but very pronounced. Now, that's a new one on me. I never thought a kid would be allergic, but there you go."

I could have hugged him. In the course of the appointment, he also called Dr. Freese to consult with her regarding her instructions on weaning Kelly from the prednisone, and they briefly discussed whether the kidney stones could be a result of the drug. Then, seeing how open he was, I told the story of Thailand and the Mystery Illness.

Dr. Kidney took a while to digest this narrative, then he cleared his throat.

"I think you have to accept that you'll never know the answer to some of this. There *is* one scenario, though, that makes sense to me. Say that when you were in Asia, Kelly was exposed to some really violent bacteria, or a wicked virus, and her immune system just revved up. But then the body didn't stop revving. It kept going and going, until eventually it started eating its own organ, in this case the liver."

At last, we'd met a doctor who wasn't afraid to be "anecdotal." He knew that I wasn't going to hold him to this theory as an official diagnosis, or expect a prescription for it. This guy seemed genuinely excited by the mysteries of medicine and the human body that we can never solve. Best of all, he seemed to have all the time in the world for us, and for Kelly's problems, and he made Kelly laugh at least half a dozen times that afternoon. We left his office more hopeful, even though in reality he'd said nothing to make us feel better—he'd even predicted that Kelly would probably have problems with kidney stones in the future—but I still found him comforting.

When I got back home in Philadelphia, I pasted the corncob water tower postcard to the wall above my desk. Every time I looked at it, I appreciated Dr. Kidney's honesty and what I came to see as the Miracle of Mayo.

We stayed in Rochester, Minnesota, for six days, and I think we tried almost every good restaurant around. The first night, at the big grand hotel, a cockroach fell out of a wine list as I opened it. Kelly wouldn't stop talking about it. We'd had brunch at the Marriott, two dinners at small bistros—one Hungarian, one French—and one evening we traveled twenty miles away to a small, quaint town filled with antiques shops, where we dined in one of those old-fashioned "country" restaurants, the kind that has the story of the founder on its menu. Kelly and I are food snobs, so I'm ashamed to say that we made fun of everything, from the Cheez Whiz that accompanied the full loaf of bread on the table all the way to the "seafood special" stuffed with "imperial crab" and doused with gobs of creamy sauce.

Still, that little country inn restaurant was nicer and more comfortable than anything else we'd had that week, and we should have been grateful. But even if we'd had four-star Michelin cuisine, I doubt we would have noticed or been impressed. The Rochester,

Minnesota, experience was all about waiting for news from Mayo, and until you get totally good news, all food is rather tasteless. By the third day of our visit, we'd already received the best news we were going to get—Kelly was over the hump, and that meant that we had to start getting her off the medication, whatever our hometown doctors might think of that. (It would be two more years until our next, more triumphant, visit to the Mayo Clinic, when Kelly was declared officially in remission from AIH. The food that time, as I recall, was like ambrosia.)

As it turns out, we could have driven back from Minnesota to Philadelphia in a shorter time than it took us to fly there, but who would have known that? How could we have expected killer thunderstorms to delay our flight for almost thirty-six hours? I remember all the hours of airport waiting through an exhausted allergy haze. My mom was the grown-up, while Kelly and I acted the parts of the spoiled traveler brats as everything went wrong. With no direct flights possible, we got seats on a plane to Cincinnati, with the promise of a connection to Philly that night. After running full speed for about a half hour at the Cincinnati airport and boarding many strange little trains, we arrived at the gate to discover that all flights into Philly had been cancelled. We ended up being bussed to an eerie gigantic motel in Coventry, Kentucky, decorated in the style of King Arthur's court, with Styrofoam shields and knights in plastic armor.

The next day we could get only a flight to Baltimore, which left late in the afternoon.

"This could be worse," said Mom.

"How?" I said.

"What if we'd gotten bad news about Kelly's health? Think about that. At least now we have hope."

Bless my mom. She always retained her equilibrium, and there I was, spiraling downward in a sullen adolescent sulk. Yes, I was happy that the Mayo folk had thought Kelly could start reducing her medications. But I had already started thinking about what a hell it would be to wean her off them, and about how I would be the one on the receiving end of most of the hell. I was working myself into a snit, forgetting the important stuff, sweating the small stuff. So what if we felt near death as we landed in violent thunderstorms in Baltimore, and so what if we had to then get to the Amtrak station and take a train to Philadelphia? We were eventually home, and in possession of better knowledge of the true state of Kelly's health than we'd had in over a year. I wish I could have had simple faith about the good things in life; I wish I could have had more of my mother's attitude.

And so we limped back to our home base, and the next day Kelly's dad drove us back to the airport to get our luggage. Chaos reigned in the baggage claim area. The airport was facing two days of delayed flights and baggage accumulation. I dreaded what I thought would be a very long process, and once I saw the overcrowded terminal filled with suitcases from scores of delayed and postponed flights, I thought we'd be there for hours. Alan had never seen the actual suitcases we'd taken for the trip, and yet somehow, that day, he walked into a terminal crowded with thousands of pieces of luggage and, within three minutes, picked ours out of the lineup. There are very few occasions in life when I can say my jaw dropped, but it did right then. To this day, I'm always talking about Alan's extraordinary savant luggage skills. Alan wasn't much help in the pinch of negotiating our daughter's health care, but, by golly, that man can pick out your suitcase from a hundred yards away!

As Alan loaded our luggage on a cart, I took his amazing accomplishment as a sign that much-needed change was about to arrive. We had finished Mayo trip number one, and the news was good. We'd had a scare, and it was over.

Kelly was going to be okay.

8. Acute to Chronic

Sometimes I wish
I could white-out
some parts of my
life, just take that
liquid paper white-out
and take it and
stick [it] on your life
where you want to
forget, and never
look back, never
have to look at all
the bad, bad things
that have happened
to my life, and just
put it all behind,
white it out now!

from a poem written by Kelly
before *she got sick, at age nine*

And so, after a very hard summer, we were back in Philadelphia, and back to the business of life once again.

Kelly and I were exhausted after the Mayo journey, but there was no time to recoup, because school was upon us. Before we knew it, she was back into the very hectic routine of seventh-grade existence, with lots of homework as well as recorder lessons, art classes, and her new favorite activity, Rock School, a wacky rock-and-roll academy where she was learning bass guitar and vocals. (The kids learned quickly and then gave concerts on various rock themes, such as The Beatles, Pink Floyd, or Southern Rock.) I thought things would become a bit more tranquil with Kelly's sportswoman days behind her, but all of that was replaced by the Year of the Bar/Bat Mitzvah, and nearly every weekend was taken up with elaborate birthday celebrations, which made the pace almost as hectic.

Funny about that sports stuff. God, how I hated jocks and anything to do with sports. But Kelly loved anything physical and was naturally athletic, like her dad. From five years old on, she'd been involved in sports during every possible season—soccer, basketball, softball, and swimming. She also spent three years smitten by horses, as so many young girls are, and even though we lived right in the middle of the city, Alan and I drove her out to the stables on the edge of town, where we'd watch her ride around and around in a ring. She never did as well as a horsewoman as she had on the soccer field, but she did win a few ribbons and got to the point where she was learning how to do the jumps.

Recently a British woman caused a stir by writing a newspaper article about how much her children bored her, but I understood exactly what she meant: This is how I feel about kids' sports. Alan signed up Kelly to play softball at the age of five in a league called T-ball, in which the kids hit balls from a stationary pillar. Al and I joked that the *T* in *T-ball* stands for *tedium,* and I struggled to get through each game by wading through the Sunday *New York Times* and then looking up occasionally to yell, "Go, team! Go, Kelly!" Apparently this was bad etiquette, since I heard through the parental grapevine that I was supposed to be watching each preschool move with rapt attention. It got worse as each weekend was taken up with countless sporting activities, and I didn't see why both parents had to go to the games. I schemed and planned to get out of my sports-parent obligations all the time, even though Kelly begged me to come.

And then Kelly's sports period was over, and she was no longer a jock. Joni Mitchell says it best: "You don't know what you've got 'til it's gone . . . "

Overnight, Kelly turned into a sick child who didn't have the energy to play sports, and I found myself driving past her old venues with tears in my eyes. Maybe by wishing so much that I wouldn't have to spend my weekends watching boring games, I'd unwittingly cursed Kelly. Once, as I drove past her old softball field near the Art Museum, I even said it aloud: "If Kelly gets well, I promise I'll go to any game she wants."

My mom saw Kelly's illness as crucial to the transformation of her personality. Beforehand, she said, Kelly was more of a team person, but afterward, since she had to develop inwardly, she was able to focus on activities that took more concentration. It's true, I guess, but I'll never know if Kelly would have become more intellectual anyway. Still, her attention span did seem to grow in leaps and bounds that first year of her illness. She started reading Renaissance English poetry, for example, and eagerly attacked Shakespeare plays instead of complaining about their difficulty. Since she could no longer run around without feeling exhausted, she began listening to music more intently, and that contributed in part to her evolution from girl jock to girl Goth rocker. Her frequent absences from school in that second half of sixth grade might have led her to have less interest in her studies, but the opposite happened: She became obsessed with deadlines and even got angry when her teachers gave her extra time to complete assignments.

School was a sore subject for me, since it turned out that Kelly's small alternative school was not really equipped to help with her health requirements. I had a problem explaining Kelly's condition to the principal and some of the teachers. They kept focusing on the *hepatitis* part of autoimmune hepatitis, worrying that Kelly was contagious. I began to get weary explaining that *hepatitis* merely meant an inflammation of the liver, and that while hepatitis A, B, and C could be contagious, an autoimmune version could not be, any more than arthritis or sinus allergies or cancer. Kelly did not have a virus; she had a condition.

"Just tell me what you need from us," her principal said early on when I called to discuss her illness. "We'll do anything for you and Kelly."

"Well," I ventured, "a major problem for Kelly is fatigue. She needs a place to lie down and rest during the day, so she can make it through the entire school day."

"We can't do that," the principal said. "We don't really have any place where she can rest."

It drives me crazy when people say they'll do anything and then, at the first request, turn you down. Why even say it? I felt real flashes of anger that this precious, overprivileged private environment couldn't scrape together one quiet place for my sick child. If we'd sent Kelly to public school, they'd be required by law to allow her to rest in the nurse's office.

The principal finally said that Kelly could come to her office and take a nap on the couch. Yeah, I thought. Kelly'll do that when hell freezes over. What sane seventh-grade student would willingly go to the principal's office?

"I'm hardly ever in there during school hours," she said, "and even if I were, I'm sure she could rest comfortably while I worked."

Of course, Kelly never did take her up on that offer. Instead, she often "pooped out" in the middle of the day and had to come home early. I tried not to be upset or angry about it, but it put a huge crimp in my day and, of course, my work. I never knew when she'd need the extra rest.

As soon as we arrived back East, I started weaning her from the prednisone. I should have called her doctors at CHOP and told them of the Mayo Clinic recommendations, but I was too cowardly. I feared what they would say, that they would tote out the big guns and threaten that I was going to kill my child by taking her off the drugs. I just didn't feel up to the challenge. So, armed with the new prescriptions from the Mayo docs, I began the arduous process of weaning Kelly all by myself.

To call the weaning process "horrible" would be too nice. It was more than horrible, yet neither she nor I expected it would be. It made sense that we initially thought we were in the clear, knowing that Kelly's dosages could be lowered. But as I've mentioned, when you're on such a high level of a steroid drug, your adrenal glands actually shut down, letting the drug do the work of regulating your metabolism and energy levels. Once you remove the drug, it takes a while for the body to get the message that it needs to pitch in again, so the side effects of weaning from prednisone are almost as bad as being on the drug. In Kelly's case, they seemed worse. She became moodier and more tired than she'd ever been. Most days she made it through school, at least until about two o'clock and sometimes for the entire day, but that was about all she could handle. She'd come home and go straight to bed, crying because she couldn't keep her eyes open long enough to concentrate on homework. She was still very interested in learning how to draw and paint, but distressed that her hands shook all the time. She found some solace at the potter's wheel, where she was the only seventh-grader skilled enough to throw pots. But however hard she worked, she couldn't attain the coordination she'd had only a year before the liver disease struck and we made our Faustian bargain with prednisone and Imuran.

At one point Kelly started actively trying to dodge even the lower dose of her drugs, claiming that she would take them when she got to school. Eventually I had to stand over her and practically force the dwindling dosages down her throat. It was horrible, and sometimes both of us would end up screaming or crying. I was frantic that she wouldn't take the right dosage, leaving herself open for even worse side effects. I began putting notes illustrated with a skull and crossbones into her lunchbox, along with the drugs that she claimed made her sick at breakfast time.

TAKE THE DRUGS OR ELSE, I would scribble beneath the pirate symbol, or, worse, *TAKE THESE DRUGS OR YOU'RE GOING TO DIE!!!* One horrible fight we had I replayed again and again in my head: Kelly said that I had made her ugly and retarded-looking by making her take the drugs.

"No boy is ever going to want me," she said, "because of how ugly the drugs make me."

"Well, it's even harder to get a date when you're rotting in a box," I hissed back, shocking myself. (Wow, Cathy, I said in a mental Valley Girl voice, "that was, like, way *harsh*.")

"My friends laugh at the notes, Mom. They think you're weird," she said one day.

I still have her class picture from that year, even though my mother begged me to throw it away. Actually, it's only the proof version of her photo, which you're supposed to return, but I never did. I certainly wasn't going to buy a picture of my kid looking like a freakazoid, with a huge bloated face and acne all over her cheeks. Whenever I see it, it takes me a minute to figure out who it is, and then, when I do, the same moan comes out of me before I can stop it. I can't tell you where the photo is now, but it has a damned sneaky way of falling out of folders or the corners of books when I least expect it to, and then I feel a catch in my throat and the familiar stinging at the edge of my eyes. That photo pops up just the way Kelly's illness did, unexpectedly, and I think it serves the same purpose: to remind me that bad things can happen quickly, but also that things can get better.

They started getting better for Kelly right away, almost as soon as I began weaning her by two milligrams of prednisone per week. It was as if her melon-head was a balloon and we were gradually letting out the air. Her body began to shrink, too, little by little. By Thanksgiving she could even fit into size-fourteen clothing. When her dad and I went to the Christmas concert at her school, and I saw her smiling face shining out from the a cappella group, the tears that came to my eyes were happy ones. Several parents, the ones who knew what we'd gone through, stopped me as we trooped out of the auditorium to say how well Kelly looked.

The goal, if everything continued well, was to have her off the prednisone completely by her birthday, which was in February, a little less than six months after we'd visited the Mayo Clinic. I did make that goal, even though I still kept her on the immunosuppressant drug

Imuran, though we both noticed how sick it made her right after she swallowed it. I finally confessed to the doctors at CHOP that I'd embraced the Mayo idea of weaning Kelly from the prednisone. But after our second follow-up appointment, the CHOP doctors made it clear that we were supposed to *decrease* the dosage, not get her off it entirely. But I had taken Dr. Czaja's suggestions as gospel, and I continued the weaning process until prednisone was off our daily regimen by Christmas of 2001. The gastroenterologists at CHOP make note of this in a letter to Kelly's pediatric practice:

> Kelly and her mother report that they discontinued her prednisone 5 mg. od dosage in December of 2001 without informing us. They did this knowingly and against our advice given on several occasions, that the sudden discontinuation of prednisone could precipitate liver crises in patients with autoimmune chronic active hepatitis.

I was willing to live with the specialists' anger, especially since I hadn't just decided willy-nilly to wean Kelly from the prednisone. Looking back at the records I saw, I notice that only once did the CHOP gastroenterology folks ever acknowledge that we'd taken the trouble to travel all the way to Minnesota to seek advice about Kelly's drug dosage. I reduced the amount of the steroids gradually, by two to five milligrams each week, as I'd been instructed at Mayo. It took over three horrible months of withdrawal to accomplish.

As usual, when it comes to chronic illness, not all Kelly's progress was upward. We had our scares, and Kelly was understandably prone to panic whenever she felt crappy. She wanted to get off the drugs, but she worried she'd have a relapse, and so did I. The Children's Hospital doctors' dire predictions were never far from my mind, and I'd often have negative daydreams about how humiliating it would be to show up at CHOP with my daughter's liver failing. *I told you so, I told you so, I told you so,* I imagined Dr. Palmer saying as they wheeled Kelly into an ambulance plane bound for Pittsburgh and a liver transplant. There were about three times that fall when Kelly felt so fatigued that she asked to go to the emergency room, but by this time we'd learned a useful trick: If you called the Gastroenterology Department and got a sympathetic soul, you could take your kid in for an "emergency phlebotomy," meaning an emergency blood test, instead of waiting for the entire medical exam at the emergency room proper. Yes, you still had to wait among the pings and bells of the Rube Goldberg–type interactive exhibits, just on the other side of the emergency area, but the wait was seldom longer than forty-five minutes, and the blood-taking lasted only seconds. By the next day, the Gastroenterology Department had the results, and in our case that fall, the results were always good. Kelly's liver numbers, which had been stable for the five months since she started the drug regimen, continued to be good.

Unfortunately, though, Kelly's kidney problem continued, and in December of that first weaning period, we found ourselves back in the emergency room because of what her medical report called "severe pain in patient's left flank." As soon as the pain hit, Kelly and I knew what it was: The damned stones were back. And here it was, only a few weeks until Christmas, and we'd have to start playing that painful waiting game again. Should she drink lots of water and try to flush the stone or stones out, or should we just have our crack surgeon go in there and get them again?

Because we knew that an operation was possible, it was hard to think about trying the more passive approach, so this time, while

Kelly was still in the hospital, her dad and I decided we should get the damned thing over with. It was harder this time, because Kelly was more familiar with how sore she'd be and how invaded she would feel "down there." But at least if she got the stones removed, she'd have a good chance of enjoying the holiday. We were also "hip" to the pain management thing, so I demanded the morphine pump once again. As hospitalizations go, this one went the smoothest any had ever gone, and in four days she was home and on the mend. When she had the procedure, she had just gotten off prednisone, which was a subject I couldn't discuss with the liver team, so it was far from pleasant to endure their rounds. Dr. Palmer avoided me altogether, and even one of her assistants, who'd been nice before, was very icy while reviewing Kelly's information. All of it still made me nervous: What if I was wrong, and they were right? What if I was playing Russian roulette with my kid's life, which is what the CHOP liver doctors must have thought I was doing? I went over and over in my head what I would do if I found out that Kelly's AIH had returned. I called my mom and asked if she would help me get Kelly out to the Mayo Clinic again, if something happened, and she assured me she would. It seemed like madness, though. Here we were, right across a bridge from one of the presumably best children's hospitals in the country, in a major city known for its excellent medical community, and all I could think of was flying my kid out to a cornfield in Minnesota for help with her disease.

Kelly's leaf collection, one of the biggest science assignments at her school, was due that December, and her teachers kept saying she didn't need to hand it in. For some reason that made her angry, so she worked on it every spare moment, even when she was hooked up to catheters and IVs. "Leaf assignment" sounds a bit flakey, but the thing was actually a very rigorous test of the students' knowledge of scientific names and facts about deciduous trees, and I was proud of Kelly that she wouldn't give up easily. In the end, her seventh-grade teacher told me that Kelly's leaf book was one of the best in the class. I'm so glad she didn't procrastinate in the collection part and was left only with assembling the book itself by the time she got so sick with the new kidney stones.

Once back home, Kelly was still plagued with all the usual prednisone problems, even though she was nearly weaned from the drug. (The whole process took until February.) Insomnia was the worst part of it, and I confess that we began to "borrow" sleeping pills occasionally from her dad. Otherwise the poor kid would have been wandering around awake every night. It's not that the doctors were unaware of the insomniac effect of the prednisone, but early in her diagnosis we'd found out that she would qualify for sleeping pills only if we submitted to a full psychiatric evaluation *and* if I'd agree to put her on antidepressants as well—Zoloft, to be precise. Kelly was never depressed, and I didn't see why she needed to go on a full-time systemic antidepressant. There is chemical depression, and then there's situational depression. I'd say that being diagnosed with Kelly's disease at the age of twelve and battling the side effects of her drugs would naturally lead to a bit of depression.

The fall after Mayo was hard, but there were major things to look forward to. As I've said, it was the crazy Year of the Bar Mitzvah. Kelly had more than twenty parties to attend for her friends who were turning thirteen. As the elaborate invitations appeared in the mail, I began buying bookstore gift cards in bulk and inexpensive party dresses. There was a sports Bar Mitzvah (actually, three of those!), a comedy Bar Mitzvah, a formal Bar Mitzvah. Our house became filled with Bar Mitzvah knickknacks, all the T-shirts and souvenirs printed with the kids' names.

Kelly is a half-breed (I'm not Jewish; her dad is). I'd never thought about the lure of the Bar Mitzvah. Years ago, when I was pregnant with Kelly, one of my book editors told me she'd felt it necessary to throw a big party for her daughter when she turned thirteen, even though they weren't Jewish. It had seemed stupid to me at the time, but that was before I knew anything about having a kid. Kelly turned thirteen in February of her seventh-grade year, and already by November I was thinking that we all needed to mark that milestone with a big party. Kelly was very excited, especially when she discovered that we would rent a place and I'd have a DJ. The plan was to make the party kid-oriented, with only a few adults invited. At the time, we had both been having a love affair with everything Japanese—karaoke, Japanese floral arrangements, and especially Japanese food (tempura and sushi!) and cool *objets* we'd discovered at a new local Japanese supermarket—so it seemed like no effort at all to pick the theme: An Evening in Tokyo.

Money was a problem, but then money was always a problem, so my mom pitched in and said she'd pay for most of it. By making it a do-it-yourselfer, with me doing the decorations and food, I could squeeze a great party out of a tiny budget. I found a beautiful nineteenth-century theater on Delancey Place, complete with four rooms for wandering, a big dance floor, a piano, and a separate barroom. Lisa, the Irish woman who'd been cleaning for us for years, agreed to be the bartender and bring along another woman to help.

The timing couldn't have been better, because Kelly was gradually beginning to look more like herself. Her moon face was shrinking, and her back hump was going down. The steroids were gradually leaving her body, and she was finally becoming what she'd always been destined to be, a lovely young woman.

There was only one problem, and that was AIH-related, too. She'd recently been to a Bar Mitzvah with a particularly lively game and dance floor, and in running away from a boy, he'd pulled at her arm and WOMP!—it ended up broken. I couldn't believe it when the Bar Mitzvah boy's mom called to tell me. It was the first time I'd gotten to write in a while, and I'd settled into my office to try to knock out an essay that was long overdue. Brittle bones are another side effect of prednisone, and I was certain that if Kelly hadn't been taking the stuff, she never would have broken her arm just because a boy tugged on it. For some reason the news made me supernaturally angry. On the way to pick her up, I called her father and insisted he come to the hospital. I was out of my mind with fury.

"It's your turn," I yelled at Alan. "I can't go into that emergency room one more damned time."

While Kelly was being discharged, we were told we had to come back in two days to get the arm cast; it was a hairline fracture of the long bone. Not that bad, actually, but when we counted out the number of weeks, it was likely that Kelly was going to still have a cast on for her very special secular Bat Mitzvah.

Otherwise, she hardly noticed the arm. I began to wonder if hairline fractures really needed to be set at all. The cast was supposed to be on for five weeks, and her birthday party date fell just four days before it was to come off. One night, in a preteen fit, Kelly told me she was ugly and still bloated from the prednisone, and she was going to look ugly for her party, too, because of the stupid cast.

"Let's try to get it off early," I said. Surely, the doctors would give her time off for good behavior, I thought. Especially for a kid who's gone through so much.

I started calling the Orthopedics Department, leaving heartfelt messages about how I hoped she could get her cast removed just a teeny-weeny bit early. I left messages for her orthopedist every day for a week. No one ever called me back. One parent I talked to said, "Hey, just go down there. I'm sure someone in that cast room will take it off for you."

And so we did. I took Kelly out of school, and we went to the Orthopedics Department bright and early, when appointments began. I explained to the receptionist that we needed to have a cast taken off, and I told them all of Kelly's doctors' names. I also dropped the names of the professionals who'd put on that cast and two others Kelly had had from sports injuries over the years.

No dice. We sat there for three hours, and it was clear that we weren't going to get anyone to help us. So I got sneaky and walked back to the cast room and lucked out. There was "Maria," a woman who had loved Kelly and had helped us in the past. I explained that Kelly was less than a week away from cast removal anyway, and beseeched her to help out a young girl about to make her "illness-free" debut at her secular Bat Mitzvah. Maria was really nice and made the requisite calls to Kelly's doctors, but no one called back. She even allowed Kelly and me to sit in the cast room, which unfortunately got our hopes up a little too much. After an hour, when not even Maria was coming around, Kelly began to get teary.

"I have to wear this ugly dirty thing to my party," she said.

"No you don't!" I said. "I'll take this cast off you myself, goddamn it." I felt like Scarlett O'Hara in that corny scene: "As God is my witness, I'll never let my daughter go ugly again!"

And then we did a Thelma and Louise. Man, it was exciting! We simply stood up and left the Orthopedics wing altogether. No one saw us, yet we felt like fugitives. I began to hum the *Mission Impossible* theme song quietly, and Kelly giggled as we made it to our car. We paid our parking fee and escaped into Center City, where I had a destination in mind: a neighborhood hardware store.

I'd been in that store only once before, for a very satisfying visit: In the spring they had flats of well-priced, old-fashioned annuals sitting by the door. Nothing fancy: just zinnias, marigolds, and portulaca. The store was one of those old-fashioned places with warped wooden floorboards and aisles filled with dusty tools and screws and nails. It even had that wonderful old-fashioned smell of wood and screws that makes a hardware store an attractive location either on a hot summer day or, as it was now, in the dead of winter. A cast of regulars, dressed in overalls and denim welding jumpsuits, come in and out, picking up a few things at a time and running a constant tab. In the front, by the cash register, at a kind of wooden platform, the customers sit while the cashier makes keys or checks prices. It reminded me of all the hardware stores I'd ever visited with my dad as a young girl, and I had a fleeting fantasy of writing one of those "you are there" types of books about what could happen in a hardware store over the course of a few months.

Kelly and I were odd characters there, in the middle of a school day, a mom and her kid in a big cast. I had promised Kelly I'd get her out of the thing, but how? I knew I needed a saw, but did I need a drill, too? And what kind of saw? Would I need, say, an ice pick to puncture holes before I tried to pry the cast open? I was totally lost.

The store's owner came back to greet me after we'd been wandering the jigsaw aisle for a while.

"What kind of a job are you trying to do?" he asked. He was a nice, prematurely balding hippie type with a big pleasant face—a bit like a young Stephen Stills.

I hesitated.

"I think I need a saw."

"I see. What kind? What kind of job are you trying to do?"

"Yeah. Well. Okay, I'm not going to lie to you. I need a saw, or something, because we want to take off her cast."

Kelly gave him a weak smile and moved her left arm upwards, tapping the cast with her right hand.

"Oh. Gee. I don't want you to have to *buy* something just to do that. I can help you with that." He smiled, and I knew he didn't have the slightest idea what he was offering. Still, I sure wasn't going to refuse.

The poor guy. It's much harder to get a cast off than anyone would think. It started well enough, with him drilling through Kelly's cast while she sat in the window, on the platform used by many of the carpenters and plumbers who waited for parts. From the beginning, the hardware store owner was the center of everything, as the handymen who frequented his shop came in and out for parts and tools, pausing only to give advice about how to "get that sucker off."

We were about forty-five minutes into the task when I realized how stupid I'd been to agree to let a stranger cut off my daughter's cast. But by then it was too late: It would have been insulting to tell him I didn't believe he could do it. The guys who wandered in and out offered many solutions, and one guy insisted that the drill he had in his truck would do the trick.

The noise! The *smell!* It was gross watching Mr. Hardware try all sorts of saws and then various drills on the hardened arm carapace. I started having nervous fantasies that a policeman would pass by and notice the little crowd of handymen assembled around Kelly. Wasn't there a law against performing medical procedures without a license?

"Did ya go to hospital?" one carpenter said.

Mr. Hardware flashed me a look.

"Well, yes," I said, "but no one came around to do the job, and she's got her birthday party in three days, and I promised her she wouldn't have to turn thirteen wearing this ugly cast."

"A birthday, honey? Ah, that's swell," said a plumber.

"I have twin babies," said Mr. Hardware, who was starting to sweat at this point. He was using a chisel and a hammer (damn, that cast was hard!) and had produced about a six-inch gash in the side of the cast, when the terrible shadow of liability crossed his face. He started swearing as he worked. He could probably see his business evaporating within a ridiculous lawsuit for which he had only himself to blame.

"Listen," he said. "Don't ever tell anyone I did this, okay? Don't ever mention it."

"Okay," I said. What the hell had I been thinking? Sure, it had seemed like a lark. But what if something went wrong? What if he pierced Kelly's skin and we'd have to return to Children's Hospital, to the emergency room, where I'd be shown up as the worst mother in the world? And what was I teaching my daughter about flouting authority?

The whole thing started not to be fun for poor Kelly about

twenty minutes before victory. When the cast finally gave way, what should have been a triumphant moment only seemed gross and sad. Kelly's arm was red and shriveled, and the smell was unbelievably foul. While Mr. Hardware didn't exactly say, "Get the hell out of here," he obviously couldn't wait until we got out the door. I tried to give him something for his trouble, but he declined vociferously.

"Really," he said. "Just don't tell anyone. Ever."

A week later I returned and left some of my books and articles for him about having babies, since he'd said he was the father of baby twins. He wasn't there. I wanted to say, "Please thank him again for taking off my daughter's cast," but of course that was out of the question. I mumbled something about how he'd done me a favor, and left it at that.

Kelly might have been upset during the last half hour or so of Project Cast Removal, but she was delighted with the result as we busied ourselves for her party. She picked out two outfits, one a cute top and jeans and the other a darling little dress from Target, a slinky number in an orange paisley, size twelve. She looked great in it and made the bold decision to get a very short haircut to go with it. That backfired a little—she was afraid afterward that she looked too boyish, but I thought she looked wonderful.

The invitations had been computer-printed on beautifully embossed rice paper. I'd scoured the city for Japanese paraphernalia, including Japanese flags we hung from everywhere, Japanese fashion magazines, classical Japanese floral arrangements, and strange Japanese candies with cooler-than-possible graphic designs. I'd even found a woman who rented out big Sumo wrestling costumes and a cloth wrestling ring so that kids could practice being two-ton Sumo guys for a while.

Of course, like every party, there were some minor problems. The DJ was late and could barely carry his equipment up the three flights of stairs, and the thirteen-year-old boys devoured tray after tray of sushi in a matter of minutes. At one point we caught a group of kids piling up on an outside balcony that looked about to collapse. But, hey, that's par for the course when anyone gets randy adolescents together. For the most part, the party was a galloping success, and Kelly, resplendent in her party dress and makeup, looked beautiful. The "bar" was also a big hit. Lisa and her co-bartender served the Cokes and other soft drinks with the little paper Asian umbrellas I'd ordered by the gross, and I'd underestimated how much fun it would be for kids to be able to sidle up to a bar and order what they wanted. Some of them left half-finished drinks everywhere as they were eager to return to the bar to order more. They also liked the rooms filled with disreputable furniture and Japanese magazines. Being allowed to wander around made them feel grown- up. A few adults hung around the bar, too. We had sake and white wine and watched the Sumo wrestling. One of the moms, Erin, embarrassed her daughter by doing a karaoke number. Unbelievably, the kids actually *ate* the Japanese candy, something I hadn't anticipated, since most of it was low-sugar, strange-tasting stuff. And Kelly and her friends had fun at the sundae bar we set up at the end of the evening.

Yes, all in all, it was a success, a kind of relaunching of Kelly onto the social scene on her own terms.

I cried when I saw the pictures from the party the next day. Kelly looked so lovely, and so happy. There was one where her good friend Sam was wrapped up in Japanese flags, running through the room, with Kelly laughing behind him. It felt so good to see her laugh. Her friends had forced her into a Sumo suit, too. Seeing her tricked out in "fake" fat with a big smile on her face somehow made up for the real imprisonment in ugliness she'd suffered over the last eighteen months.

The party was a huge hit among Kelly's friends because, as one of them said, "there was none of the religious stuff. We just partied. It was all about the party." And it was all about Kelly. What a crybaby I'd become, one of those moms who becomes over-sentimental at the slightest thing. Yet having people tell you your kid is on the verge of dying can do that to a cynical old broad.

How long is it before the gratitude that your kid is safe wears off? I'd like to say never, but I can tell you it's actually about a year. Once you've gone through a year *after* the terrible mess, when you see a bunch of healthy milestones and your kid doesn't end up in the emergency room, you begin to relax. Not only that, you begin to think the whole thing was a dream, and it's easier to understand why others didn't take you seriously when you told them how sick your kid was. Having a sick kid is not natural, and when your child's health returns, you're the first to embrace it, even though certain doubts remain.

Once, after Kelly had been sick for over a year, I spoke at a conference in Harrisburg, Pennsylvania, reuniting with some friends I'd met during the scary period of Alan's rehabilitation for brain injury. Nora, one of Alan's caseworkers for a state disability office, had discovered that her son was ill with leukemia at about the same time Kelly was diagnosed with AIH. He beat the illness, despite the fact that he was diagnosed with the "worst" type of leukemia. Nora was there during my speech, smiling up at me as I spoke, but then leaving briefly to take a cell phone call. After the question-and-answer session, she approached me.

"I'm sorry, but I have to drive home to my son now." She called me three days later to say that her boy was okay; he had just been running a fever, and in the post-leukemia world, that was a definite no-no. There was no way Nora could comfortably hang around a conference while thinking that her son's leukemia might have returned. Her predicament was so familiar to me. Her son might be "recovering," but the threat that he could die would never leave her, or her family. We talked later on the phone about the peculiar position of mom caregivers. While she wanted to believe that her son had beaten *it*, that he was one of the lucky ones, there was another part of her that always waited for the other shoe to drop. I'd seen her during one of those moments. There was no denying it: We were both in it for the long haul. Once you've been touched by illness, you never escape. I thought maybe that this caseworker, who'd been trained to counsel damaged families, would deal with this better than I did, but she says she does not. She just keeps her head down and goes forward, like the rest of us. I hate people who quote that Alcoholics Anonymous slogan "One day at a time," because it seems so obvious, but there are certain situations in life where that's just about all you can do, and having a kid with a chronic illness is one of them.

My friend's son is still alive, but that doesn't mean that Nora won't still flip out every time he feels a little crummy. The Sick Mommy role is just an exaggerated version of the usual maternal shtick. I talk to mothers who haven't had a toddler around in fifty years who still freeze in their steps when they hear a child yell, "Mommy!" The Sick Mommy is just the same, but she has even more reasons to worry.

9. Hold the Mayo, Full Speed Ahead

A specialist is a man who knows more and more about less and less.

Dr. Charles Mayo

Because Kelly was adamant that she didn't want to go to Mayo ever again, I worried that our second trip to the clinic of the cornfields would be a disaster. Instead, the journey turned into a magical experience, with everything going more smoothly than the first time.

Of course, circumstances were far different: The first time, we had been seeking answers. On this trip we just wanted confirmation that Kelly's bout with AIH was over for the time being. We didn't feel nearly as helpless. Since all her blood tests had been great, this trip to Mayo would be more like a rubber stamp of approval than a nervous request for a physical exam. And it helped knowing the ropes as far as a quick trip to Minnesota goes. Best of all, we were combining our trip with a speech I was giving at the Mayo Clinic about the effects of brain injury on family members. That meant I would be getting paid to appear at the clinic, and that our hotel and car would be covered. We even got to stay at the Marriott, which was the nice fancy hotel that hadn't depressed us the first time around.

We arrived at the Minneapolis airport in the early evening and were given an upgrade for a rental car because all the small autos were gone. We laughed as we saw the "boat" we would steer around Rochester for the next week, a Lincoln Town Car four times the size of any car I'd ever driven. We once again set off for the Mall of America, but not to shop: We were looking for an upscale restaurant that would enable us to avoid going into downtown Minneapolis. We found one, a kind of New Age steak and chop house with wonderful fish dishes and, for me, a great selection of wine by the glass. It was probably a chain, but a classy one decorated with wooden panels and with a lively classical music CD playing in the background. But before sitting down to gorge ourselves on an early supper of fish and garlic mashed potatoes, we hit a record store and bought three greatest hits collections: Simon and Garfunkel, Crosby, Stills, Nash, and Young, and Elton John. By the end of the week we'd be sick to death of all the tracks on the albums, but as we made our way westward along the highway, we sang along and watched the beginnings of a beautiful sunset that then was disturbed by a sudden, violent thunderstorm.

Going to the Mayo feels like a special pilgrimage, because the place is far removed from the rest of the world. It's not very easy to get to Rochester, Minnesota, from Philadelphia. Even though this was our second time, I still wasn't prepared for the oddness of the journey. Driving from Minneapolis to Rochester, you quickly end up on the Road to Nowhere. The huge Minnesota sky dwarfs your car, and the gaudy billboards stand in stark relief to the enormous sky and the golden fields stretching out endlessly. Most of the roads coming onto the highway are made of dirt.

It was the end of June, just past the longest day of the year, so it seemed to take forever for the sun to set, and right before it did, we saw our corny miracle, a glimmering pastel rainbow that seemed to hover in the enormous sky right above the city of Rochester as we came to the end of the stretch of highway.

So I can begin this part of the story with a rainbow. I'm not making it up: A big, sloppy rainbow appeared in front of our rental car as we drove across the Minnesota Plains to the Mayo Clinic for the second time. We were seeking doctors who could tell us if Kelly's liver was still being attacked by the wacko t-cells in her blood. Was she going to live or die? That very issue was always with us that year, two and a half years after she was first diagnosed with the potentially fatal disease.

The rainbow on Highway 151 was the most beautiful I'd ever seen, splashing out across a huge Minnesota sky. The diffracted pastel light gave me a sense of optimism. Everything was going to turn out okay.

Even Kelly, the jaded teen, said the rainbow was cool. She usually hates it when I talk about the sky. Sky-gazing is one of my embarrassing middle-aged obsessions, so of course she has to ridicule it. It's her job as a teenager. "The sky!" she'll yell, imitating my voice. "Oh, *darling,* look at the *SKY*!"

"This whole thing might have a happy ending," Kelly said this time, gazing at the rainbow. "Then you could write about it. I know I said you shouldn't, but maybe you should."

"I am just a poor boy, though my story's seldom told."

There in the car, as we listened to Simon and Garfunkel's greatest hits on the CD player, I told my kid that our saga of sickness and remission should begin with the rainbow.

"It's pretty corny," she said, "even though it might be true."

Why are things that are true often too corny for words? When we found out that Kelly was okay, one of my most cynical friends said, "You do realize that the damned rainbow was a total coincidence?" Ah, reality. But are we just supposed to ignore poignant symbols, even when they hit us in the face, or on the windshield?

The first time we drove to the Mayo Clinic from Minneapolis with my mother, I had been filled with trepidation and doubt. "So this is where my kid is going to be saved?" I remember thinking. But the second time, when we were traveling there to confirm that she *had* been saved, I felt an almost religious form of ecstasy. I'm an atheist, but I'm not ashamed tell you what I was thinking on that second drive from Minneapolis to Rochester: "Please, God, wherever you are, grant me a good old-fashioned case of Midwestern hokeyness. Give me a rainbow, goddamn it!"

As a speaker, I am always criticizing myself, not wanting to appear too maudlin. But two days later, when I stood before a Mayo audience to talk about our family's experience with Alan's brain injury, I allowed myself some sentimentality. I began the speech with a paean to the clinic itself, where just the day before the doctors had confirmed that Kelly was officially in remission. Shamelessly, I shared the rainbow story with my audience, and they reacted in a sentimental way, with applause and oohs and aahs. I didn't know how to feel about it. I hate speakers who manipulate the audience with stock images such as rainbows and puppies and kittens. But in another way, I knew I wasn't faking anything about how I felt about the Mayo Clinic or Rochester, Minnesota. The doctors, nurses, and even administrative assistants at Mayo had given us more hope than anyone else I'd even encountered at any other hospital.

This time I got to see my friend Jim Malec again, the one who was so supportive the first time and who had enabled us to see Albert Czaja. Jim was a smiling presence during my two speeches, something I appreciated, since I'd initially thought I was giving only one speech, with an informal session afterward. I totally "winged" my second speech, given once again from the lectern in a formal-sounding way. I can't remember now exactly what I said, but it went better than my first-hour prepared speech, since it consisted of so many things I'd had to leave out of the more formal presentation. I focused on the effects of brain injury on the immediate family of the TBI survivor, a topic near and dear to me. I was pleased that no one seemed to notice that I was more prepared for the question-and-answer session than for the speech that followed it, and that some people actually stayed for the second presentation.

Fortunately, Kelly stayed in the hotel room and slept through my two speeches, one television and radio appearance, and two print interviews. I hadn't wanted her to see me as a sentimental slob, although afterward I realized that I'd missed my one opportunity for her to witness me as a brain injury expert. I called her from the Marriott lounge at lunchtime, and she came down to meet me and two of the brain injury "friends" I'd met over a vast Internet support list. They were amused to see that Kelly was still in her pajamas, and we joked about her being the typical American teenager. Kelly and I didn't have any more appointments for two days, although she'd already had all the tests and scans she would need, and the kidney specialist's office had told me that her liver results were normal, so the rest of our appointments, which would take place in a few days, somehow seemed unnecessary.

Killing time seemed more fun this visit than before, maybe because I'm a lazy gal who doesn't mind getting a very late start on the day, not unlike a teenager. We had our Lincoln Town Car boat, and we decided to use it to its fullest extent. Each day, a little after lunchtime, we'd take off for what we hoped would be interesting locations. Of course, I insisted on seeing the corncob water tower again, but that took all of twenty minutes. We revisited the country inn restaurant where we'd gone with my mom, and started exploring the side roads out of Rochester. It seemed to take about five and a half miles before minor highway tributaries turned into tiny dirt roads dotted with Amish farms. We were shameless tourists, noticing how the electricity lines halted and broke off before they got to these farms, and how much bigger the Amish barns were than the houses. We got to like a few roads and began stalking the teenage boys who would come out of the driveways in their horse-drawn buggies.

I should be embarrassed to talk about this, but I think every mother of a teenage girl has exhibited this behavior: In order to really enjoy the day, I had to "get into" stalking the Amish buggies with Kelly. We tried not to be too obnoxious, but as soon as we spotted one, we would slow down our Lincoln and travel at a respectable distance as we speculated on the cuteness of the driver. Then, summoning our courage and watching the road for a good time to pass, we'd pull up alongside and travel by the little buggy, almost always driven by the world's cutest long-haired blond teenage boy. The first few times, Kelly was shy, but sometime during the second day when we were doing it, she began to wave, and then to worry when her attempts to make contact went unnoticed.

"He wouldn't even look at me," she said one time.

"Of course he wouldn't look at you. He's Amish. And we're gawking. He's not going to acknowledge you at all. We shouldn't even be doing this."

But Kelly would not be satisfied. In her mind, there was some *Romeo and Juliet* teen movie plot lurking in which a cute blond Amish boy would glimpse her countenance and fall deeply in love with her. I'm sure it involved dramatic scenes at the Mayo Clinic, too, with the horse and buggy tied up outside the emergency room.

Kelly was fourteen and a half, the age when you are just dying to discard your "youth" and try new things. Going to a world-famous clinic with her mother in a hick area was not one of her goals, so she kept trying to bend our time there toward her desires.

"Why can't I drive?" she said on the first day we were traveling up the highway toward Rochester.

"Because you don't have a license," I said.

"Why don't you let me drive anyway?" she asked on the second day, and then again on the third. We had driven that day out to the Mississippi River, to a little beach I'd read about, and were returning sunburned and water-weary at dinnertime, exploring yet again the dirt Amish byways. I hadn't seen another car for the last thirty minutes.

I pulled over a few feet and stopped the Lincoln under a low-lying tree, then turned off the ignition.

"Drive, then," I said.

The color seemed to drain from her face.

"What?"

"You heard me. If you want to do it that badly, then do it. Drive, kid."

As I got out of the driver's seat and scuffed along the dusty road along the back of the car, I felt my bowels shift. What the hell was I doing? Bad mom, Cathy! Bad mom!

But now I was into my bluff, and Kelly took about a quarter the time I did to get into the driver's seat. I made a big, ostentatious show of buckling my seat belt and a mock sign of the cross.

"Mom!" she said. "Maybe I shouldn't do it."

"No. Do it," I barked. "There's no one here. What are going to do, run over a buggy?"

I hoped I appeared more confident than I felt. The sound of crashing metal and screeching tires flashed through my imaginative hearing system. A flash of me on the cell phone to the car rental company floated through my future image file.

They say that giving birth is the most amazing day of your life, and it's certainly up there in the top ten. But I'd also like to add the day your kid takes her first steps, or the wonderful moment when a child leaves your arms to swim independently for the very first time. I'll never forget that empty feeling in my arms when Kelly kicked away from me in our community swimming pool and thrashed to the side all on her own. And I'll never forget that day on the dirt road in Minnesota when Kelly tentatively put her foot on the gas and eased us on our way. It brought back the complicated rush that driving entails. How do you measure your acceleration versus your braking? How do you watch everything out of each side and then figure out how much you have to slow down to make a turn? How do you remember to put on your turn indicator? All of this was second nature to me after thirty years of driving, but it was a wild new world to Kelly. Still, she seemed born to the life of the road. She'd been a motorhead since she was two, always wanting to sit behind the wheel in parked cars and pretend to drive. When she was only eighteen months old, she sat in our friend Mark's fancy Mercedes and said over and over, "Gwanma cah" (Grandma's car), because my mother at the time had owned an entry-level baby Benz, and Kelly recognized the instrument panel. The kid just couldn't wait to drive, and of course I shouldn't have allowed it at fourteen, but somehow, all of Rochester, Minnesota, seemed our oyster, and I wanted her to do something daring and different to mark her passage into wellness.

I regretted it a lot after that first day, because each time we went out she asked to drive again. I only let her do it two more times, but once, another car came by and she panicked a bit, and another time she got flustered when I yelled at her to put on her turn indicator. On the third and last time I allowed it, we actually saw a FedEx truck, and that was too damned civilized for me. The drive was never as simple or magical as that first day, but that's true of so many "firsts" in life. As Baby's First Drive has grown in stature as a myth in my head and among (often disapproving) friends and family members, I've laughed to myself that a kid who was raised in a one subcompact family should have her first driving experience in a giant Lincoln Town Car on dirt roads in Minnesota.

Upon arriving back in Rochester, I saw a cute little trailer parked in the lot of a shopping mall decorated with paintings of strawberries, with a line in front of it and a sign promising fresh local strawberries.

"Let's stop," I said to Kelly, who moaned as she always does when she wants to get home and plunk herself in front of the television set.

"No," she said. "I don't want strawberries."

"Since when? They're your favorite fruit."

"They're gonna suck," she said as I pulled into the lot. "Look, they have dirt all over them," she carped as I returned to the car with a giant flat (the minimum amount I could purchase).

"Trust me," I said. "These will be the best strawberries you will ever eat."

The hotel valet parking guy smirked when he saw us come out of the car with sticky fingers and smeared lips carrying our dirty strawberries over to the hotel elevator bank. Back in the room, we continued gorging ourselves to the point where we didn't make it out for dinner, ordering room service hamburgers at ten when our fructose high wore off.

It was nice to feel like Mayo alumnae, and all of our visits seemed like Old Home Week. Dr. Freese was delighted with Kelly's progress, but we never did get to see Dr. Czaja the second time around. Dr. Kidney greeted us with more corny jokes. I'd been obsessing with schistosomiasis, a disease I thought Kelly could have contracted in the floating markets of Thailand. Could her body still be harboring snail egg parasites? The kidney doctor got us hooked up with an infectious disease specialist at the clinic, who did further tests to see if Kelly had been challenged by parasites and not beset upon by AIH.

The infectious disease specialist was a breath of fresh air. She took a person's right to travel to medically dangerous places as God-given and gave us a lot of advice about what every traveler, and especially every woman, should bring along on journeys to the third world, or even just to Europe. These included basic antibiotics, an antidiarrheal medicine, and anti-yeast infection cream—which weren't that exotic and all made sense. She was the first doctor to talk to me about the teenager's vulnerability to meningitis, and I made a mental note to get Kelly inoculated against it before she went off to college. Yet after a variety of tests, the infectious disease specialist could not find anything indicating that Kelly might have been infected by snail parasites, although she did note that all traces of such an incident might have disappeared from Kelly's tissues long ago. She was also very disparaging about the quality of the biopsy samples taken at Children's Hospital. She and the kidney doctor professed astonishment that the samples had not been prepared for the study of infectious disease, even though I had told CHOP about our trip to Thailand again and again. By not preparing the samples for such a study, the doctors at CHOP had effectively cut off that line of inquiry from the very beginning. I still wonder why. If I were a doctor, I'd find that an exciting possibility because of the unusual nature of the case and also because it would have meant a very different long-term prognosis for Kelly. If, indeed, Kelly's revved-up autoimmune system was caused by a parasite, we'd be in a different position. She'd be the victim of a parasite rather than a person with an autoimmune disease.

Still, why would I prefer to think that I'd exposed my kid to a terrible parasite instead of accepting that she was afflicted by an autoimmune disease such as AIH? AIH is a serious condition with an 80 percent chance of recurrence, so I suppose that by clinging to the idea that Kelly had had a one-time bizarre reaction to some bacteria or parasite while were in Asia, I could believe that her health ordeal was a fluke and not an unexplainable deadly disease. We have no serious history of autoimmune disease in our families, so why would this happen to our otherwise healthy kid? So I've always walked the line, unsure of what the hell happened. The hardest thing to accept is that we might never know. I find this so bizarre, that in our world of modern diagnosis, there are still situations that remain a mystery, but apparently the liver, of all organs, harbors the most mysteries.

Andrew Corsello, the writer who so generously shared his experiences with liver disease with me when Kelly was first diagnosed, has accepted that he might never know what caused his own liver failure. One day he was hiking up a mountain with his four-year-old stepsister on his back; the next he was lying in a bed in total liver failure. His doctors say that somehow his body became stressed and got the signal to destroy his liver, but they'll never know why.

"When you start to get into the liver stuff," he told me on the phone one day when I'd told him that Kelly's liver numbers were going down, "it will blow your mind. People's livers fail all the time, and no one knows why. Your body can just go haywire, and when it does, it can decide to start destroying organs. I get really scared thinking about how it could even be coming from the environment."

I suppose it makes sense that the liver, the sturdy "workhorse" of the human organs, seems to have a mysterious Achilles' heel that we can't yet understand. It is the only organ that can take vast amounts of abuse and will regenerate over time, and yet when it goes, it does so in a very dramatic way. Gastroenterologists, nurses, and even laypeople will speak of the liver "crashing."

If I had to pick the oddest part of Kelly's illness, I'd say it was this uncertainty. Her bout with AIH was swift and rather vicious, as was her struggle with the prednisone and Imuran. It really did seem like a horrible accident rather than an episode of chronic illness. And now, two years after it started, it seemed officially over, with the Mayo doctors telling her to go away, to live well and prosper.

For the most part, we have. Kelly has tried to take Dr. Czaja's wonderful advice to remove AIH from the front of her brain and put it at the very back, and to live life to the fullest and try not to worry about AIH. As I'm writing this, she is eighteen, and because we moved away from Philadelphia to Los Angeles during her second year of high school, many of her friends don't even know that she ever suffered from an autoimmune disease. She is always embarrassed when I have to reveal it to people, as I did when she traveled to Uruguay with her classmates in her junior year. (Whenever Kelly travels anywhere exotic, she needs to be aware of where to go and how to act if her liver crashes out.) The principal of her school, who accompanied the students on the trip, was surprised to find that Kelly had once been so ill. Everyone always is, because she is now the picture of robust health: a big, rosy-looking girl who looks more like a plump Renaissance Madonna than an MTV chick.

But some traces of AIH and the drugs remain. Prednisone definitely forever left its mark on Kelly's body, both in good and bad ways. Her hair turned auburn, a strange side effect that most women would kill for. (Almost daily people ask her where she gets her highlights, and if we're together we wink at each other and chuckle. From the support lists I've heard about differences in hair texture and color from cortisone, and also voice changes, which Kelly didn't suffer.) Since she was going through puberty right as the AIH hit, she also has side effects stemming from breast development. The fatty deposits that gave her the hump on her back have gradually gone down, although she has unusually large arms for her size, which causes her agony in trying on certain blouses. At the height of the prednisone poisoning, she was covered with purple stretch marks across her abdomen, arms, and thighs; for the most part these have faded. But the real problem has been with one of her breasts, which is still slightly deformed. Kelly has two choices in a brassiere: Either she gets a C cup and "smooshes" her strange D-cup breast up and into the smaller cup, or she gets a D and lets the "normal" breast swim in a lot of fabric. Whichever way, there is no traditional bra cup that can work for her, and of course she suffers from a lack of self-esteem about her altered shape, and I worry that she will suffer unduly.

I'm not the type of mom who encourages plastic surgery, but ever since this side effect to Kelly's breasts developed, I've said that one day we would get a correction for her. As I write this, we've already been turned down once by our insurance company, which refuses to believe that the corrective surgery is anything but cosmetic. I can't even think about it without feeling my blood boiling. The idea that the medical system thinks my kid should suffer unnecessary disfigurement after all the rest of the things she has suffered seems to be the final indignity in her struggles with prednisone. Luckily, she has lost even more weight so that the size discrepancy are not as noticeable. She is a beautiful young woman. Still we *will* get it fixed if she wants to. It's bad enough that Kelly had to lose some of her youth to an autoimmune disease, but if it's possible to correct the physical consequences, then we will do it, and will get the money any way we can.

The dreaded AIH left its mark in another way, too: constant fear. Anytime Kelly gets tired or feels nauseated, our minds go immediately to the disease, and instead of making us closer, it has just made us angry.

Last summer Kelly called me from Arkansas, where she was traveling cross-country with friends. They'd already been to a Woodstocklike music festival, Bonnarroo, in Tennessee, where they'd camped with eighty thousand other music fans. Kelly had hated it, and called to say that their tent was a half-hour walk from the main stage, and that it was hot as hell and there was no good food and not much to do between concerts. Now she was calling ostensibly to tell me about their trip to Memphis, but she stopped me cold as I tried to ask her about what they'd been seeing and how they'd been eating.

"Mom, listen. I have something important to tell you. I called for a reason."

Kelly has always done this; she has a way of making me feel as if I've been wasting her time all along, that chatting with Mom is not high on her agenda. I felt some trepidation about what this could be about.

"My side, the place near my liver, hurts. It hurts a lot. Today I had to stop driving because there was too much pain. What should I do? Should I go to an emergency room?"

"Well, yes, or a walk-in clinic. You know the drill. You need a blood test, liver panels."

"But I'll be back in Philadelphia in just another week. Isn't that time enough?"

I sighed. This was another part of the drill. Kelly would panic and tell me she thought her AIH was back, and yet she didn't really want to do anything to find out if it was the case.

"Kell, what can I tell you? Now you have me worried. If you just go and get a blood test, you can be sure." I knew she was embarrassed to do this in front of her three traveling companions. In the end, I knew I wouldn't be able to talk her into it. Why, then, had she told me? I guess she wanted me to just make it go away, to use magical thinking again. Or maybe, by transferring the fear to me, she could let go of it and continue on her way.

Now she was getting mad. "Mom, just forget it. Forget I said it."

Yeah, right. Forget it. Every night while she was on her road trip, I lay awake wondering if this was it, if *it* was coming back. I'm still waiting for her to get to a doctor in Philadelphia, too. And superstition certainly plays a part in all this—my fear that Kelly's disease will return has increased since I began writing this book about her. And, as I'm getting to the end, I fear that the situation will somehow change, that I won't be able to end on a high note of relief, but with a nagging theme of the inevitability of recurrence. Every time I go on to my Liver Support Group list, I worry about my hubris: Every day I read about recurrences of AIH, and yet my child has been spared. People all around us are getting liver transplants, or going on increased dosages of the dreaded prednisone, yet Kelly seems to be walking through the minefield unharmed. We are so lucky, it makes me sheepish about writing messages on the board. Kelly is still prone to "urinary weakness" from her kidney stones, and of course she battles with body image, but we've gotten off almost scot-free in terms of any lasting damage. How could we have been be so lucky? Of course, the flip side of that question is always, How could we have been so *unlucky* that she contracted this disease in the first place?

As the Year of Living Dangerously fades into personal history, there are more and more people who don't know how sick Kelly was when she was twelve, and that's just fine with her, and with me, too.

And even the people who did know didn't really understand our daily worries about Kelly's health. At the end of seventh grade, things had gotten good enough that Alan and I could consider allowing Kelly to take a class trip to Cuba.

I was apprehensive about Cuba, and I had sent her off warning her to get treatment immediately if she felt any lower back pain or any urinary abnormalities. I *should have* sent along prophylactic antibiotics, which is what I do now whenever Kelly travels, since any kind of stress seems to trigger urinary problems for her. She did have problems in Cuba, but fortunately she got excellent care and a regimen of sulfa antibiotics that knocked out her bladder infection in a matter of days. She and her teachers had called me about it, and I had to work overtime not to freak out thinking about her in a Cuban medical ward. A few of the other girls got into digestive distress, so Kelly wasn't the only kid who had to see a doctor.

Alan and I were excited at the airport waiting for Kelly's plane to come in from Miami. Finally she emerged from behind the barrier like a sixties movie diva, wearing a white chiffon scarf over her hair and large retro sunglasses. (Evidently she'd picked up a love of everything retro in Cuba, especially 1950s and 1960s cars, and she'd decided she was going back to buy a vintage auto for her first car.)

Kelly rushed up to us and air-kissed us on both cheeks, a regular Junior Gina Lollobrigida. Then she disappeared into the crowd of her classmates waiting for their luggage. A fellow mom approached and we began to catch up on what had happened that spring. This mother is an artist with a bad procrastination problem; any little thing throws off her work.

"Well, I haven't been working much because of the second dog, the new puppy," she said.

Alan and I hadn't been filled in on the new puppy, but we'd watched as this woman used her first dog to stay out of her artist's studio.

"Yeah, we got another poodle, but he got so sick. He even had to take steroids. He took prednisone, and the side effects have made him a nightmare."

"Gee, that's what Kelly took, prednisone," I said, looking knowingly at Alan.

"No! You never told me that," said the mother.

"Yes. Yes, I did. That's why she gained so much weight, and started looking weird. You remember. She was in Children's Hospital five times last year."

The woman's face was blank, and we were saved by Kelly, who had found one of her suitcases bumping around the carrousel. I was fuming, surprised that the artist mom couldn't see the steam coming out of my ears. All I could think about were the many mornings at the doggie park when I'd told her about Kelly's illness and the drugs she had to take. I guess she hadn't been listening.

"Goddamn it, she knows Kelly was sick, and then she goes spouting off about her fucking *dog* on prednisone," I mumbled to Alan as Kelly scampered around the baggage area hugging her classmates goodbye.

"Crimmins, give it up. No one is going to care like you," said Alan, and he was right.

Years ago I had an editor who'd nursed her father through two strokes and one horrible accident that resulted in further neurological damage. She told me that she would always remain haunted by the time she spent in the hospital at her father's side.

"Now whenever I pass by a hospital or clinic, I think about the Other Life—the people who are in there, existing in a kind of twilight while the rest of us go about our daily activities," she told me once in her office. "It's weird. We're out here, doing our normal stuff, and they are leading parallel lives, existing in another world where they sit with their loved ones day after day, waiting for word from teams of doctors. It's the closest to an underworld I've ever encountered."

Since Kelly's illness, I now understand what my editor meant. I sometimes feel like Orpheus returning from the underworld—Orpheus without the magical harp. I somehow got out of that hospital underworld environment, dragging Kelly with me, and it makes no sense to try to convey to others what it meant to be there. I've always had plans to go back, to right the wrongs I saw with the Children's Hospital system, or even just to bring less boring magazines into the waiting rooms. But in reality I never want to go back—in fact, to survive, I have to repudiate the experience altogether. My kid is all right now, so why relive the experience?

But I can't help holding on to it in some way. I take Kelly and her friends to a McDonald's for a McFlurry, and all of a sudden I am back at CHOP, fetching the damned Oreo Flurry up to Kelly's bleak room once again. I flip the channels to Animal Planet, and I think of all those hours watching little squirrels and guinea pigs and rabbits being resuscitated as Kelly and I waited for her latest biopsy results or as I held her hand while she was in screaming pain that not even morphine could erase. The Sick Mommy experience is always there, lurking in the background, making my love for my child and my appreciation for her survival loom large in a way I don't think it ever can for parents who've never had these scares.

If, as some wise people say, death is one way that the human experience is sharpened, if mortality is the goading condition that makes us appreciate the joys and even the sorrows of our temporal world, then surely having had a sick child is the best insurance against nonchalance. Kelly's liver and gall bladder have shrunk down again, as has my fear of losing her, but I will never be totally free of that fear, which sharpens my appreciation for her. I could say it's a gift, but that sounds cliché—yet anyone who has tried to survive the scorn and general bad attitude of a teenage girl knows that it never hurts to have extra motivation for taking abuse!

The best thing to be said about heightened experiences such as Kelly's illness is that they truly *are* heightened, an emotional favor the world does for all humans, especially parents. Even if her bout with AIH had lasted for five years instead of just two, I never would have accepted it as the norm. It was easier to see it as a strange blip in an otherwise normal life (which is really weird, because that meant it was preceded by the even weirder blip of her dad's accident). But isn't that the way life is? I've talked to lots of people about how we often feel as if we are caught in the middle of a bad television movie. So many things in life don't feel real, and as long as we feel we are careening through a surreal human landscape, we can protect ourselves from reality. Sure, I can believe that Kelly might have died, but I don't think I ever did accept it. I couldn't, because believing that a child will die simply isn't in a mom's job description, even for a woman who thinks of herself as Sick Mommy.

Acknowledgments

I will never be able to remember everyone who encouraged me to tell this story, or every wonderful person who helped our daughter in her journey through the dark days of her illness. If you are one of the many kind people who touched our lives during that time, please accept my humble blanket of thanks.

More specifically, I'd like to thank all the medical professionals and hospital staff who helped Kelly—nurses, technicians, phlebotomists, doctors, janitors, receptionists, and teachers. I know I often seem an anti-hospital curmudgeon, but in addition to the stinkers, I have met scores of wonderful medical people who truly care about their patients' welfare, and who often perform thankless, underpaid jobs. I salute these folks! I was especially impressed by everyone at the Mayo Clinic in Rochester, Minnesota, and I want to thank that institution for existing. I recommend it for anyone stumped by a spectacular health problem who wants humane, cooperative solutions. Thank you, James Malec, for helping my family to get there and see the proper people. Thanks also to everyone who visited us during our CHOP stays and brought us food and other provisions and knickknacks, including Erin and Maddy Wieand, Kay Dowgun, Robin Warshaw, Jimmy Schank, Barry Bergen, Valerie and Jordan Blum, and all our other kind neighbors and friends, especially the Lambertville brigade, Elizabeth Simon and Joan Stack. Thanks also to Lisa McDevitt.

Kelly's self-appointed godmothers, Joanne and Sarah Babaian, helped us get through this ordeal, and her third fairy godmother, Joellen Brown, has not only helped with Kelly but also with the story itself, advising me and keeping up my spirits as I relived the bad times. Joellen and Anne Kaier read the manuscript in progress—thanks! Kelly's father, Alan Forman, has been wonderfully supportive, helping me gather hospital records and other information pertinent to the story. He has always been the type of friend a writer needs, and there is not a project I have done that hasn't benefited from his kindness. Tom O'Leary, too, has been more instrumental than he knows in helping me get the story on the page.

A very big thank-you goes to my agent, Susan Raihofer, of the David Black Agency, who encouraged me to explore this episode of my life even though it seemed a daunting and terrifying prospect at first. Every author needs a staunch advocate who believes in her work, and Susan has always been there for me. Thanks also to Anne Merrow, who first brought this story to Thomas Dunne Books, and to Marcia Markland, who has been a very gracious and supportive editor. Her patience has been inspiring! Diana Szu has shepherded the manuscript through the entire process.

This book absolutely had to be dedicated to my kid, Kelly, an astounding and talented young woman. I want to thank her for agreeing that I could tell her story.

Finally, there is my mom, Betty Lancaster, who keeps me afloat in so many ways. She took care of me through a recent terrible illness that threatened to destroy my work altogether, and for that, and for so many other things, I am thankful. She, more than anyone, was with me through Kelly's battle with AIH, and I don't think I could have summoned the strength to minister to my daughter without my mother's soothing presence. My heart goes out to everyone battling autoimmune illness of any kind. Let's hope that someday science will eradicate the flaws in the human body that can allow such terrible suffering.

About the Author

Cathy Crimmins has written or co-written twenty-two books, most recently the award-winning memoir *Where Is the Mango Princess?* and the pop culture history *How the Homosexuals Saved Civilization.* She is also an award-winning educational screenwriter and has worked as a consultant for science museums across the country. She has taught writing at the University of Pennsylvania and has spoken all around the county. Her daughter, Kelly, is now a college student.